Gardens Without Boundaries

Gardens Without Boundaries

Paul Cooper

MITCHELL BEAZLEY

Gardens Without Boundaries
Paul Cooper

First published in 2003 by Mitchell Beazley,
an imprint of Octopus Publishing Group Ltd,
2–4 Heron Quays, London E14 4JP

ISBN 1 84000 738 9

A CIP catalogue copy of this book is available from the British Library

Commissioning Editor: Michèle Byam
Executive Art Editor: Christie Cooper
Contributing Editor: Jo Weeks
Design: Holger Jacobs/Mind
Production Controller: Sarah Rogers
Picture Researcher: Sarah Hopper
Indexer: Sue Farr

Printed and bound in China by
Toppan Printing Company Limited

half-title page: garden in Chile/
design Juan Grimm
title page: garden in Palm Springs,
California/design Steve Chase
contents page: garden in California/
design Topher Delaney
endpapers: garden in Auckland,
New Zealand/design Ted Smyth

Contents

Introduction

Over the centuries, the creators of gardens have been concerned with the relationship between their creations and the surrounding landscape. In their work garden designers have sought to conceal or blur the boundary that defines a garden, to extend the garden into the landscape beyond, or to "borrow" that landscape so that it becomes an extension of the garden, and these ideals continue to occupy them to the present day. Some contemporary designers are adopting and adapting traditional devices and re-working them with the benefit of modern materials and construction methods. Others, who belong more to the world of art than horticulture, are extending the boundaries in a conceptual way, challenging the meaning of the word "garden".

From its early beginnings, garden design has evolved in two main directions. In one, gardens have been hidden behind walls or enclosed within buildings. This tradition can be traced back as far as the fifth century BC to Greece, where private houses contained courtyard gardens. By the third century BC, the idea had been adopted as a blueprint for the peristyle garden of the Roman villa, which consisted of a central ornamental garden surrounded by columns and a covered walkway. The Islamic residential gardens of the seventh and eight centuries were mainly courtyards, a tradition that migrated to Moorish Spain, where it is

best represented by the Alhambra in Granada, which has several garden courts. In Japan, Zen gardens of raked gravel and carefully positioned stones are still built within walled courtyards or even inside the house. The enclosed garden tradition continues today, finding favour in high-density urban environments, where gardens are often designed as an integral part of the architecture.

The other direction in garden design has been taken by designers whose quest has been to extend boundaries, both in reality and imagination, and to connect the garden with a wider landscape. In Europe, this type of garden was first seen in the Italian Renaissance villa and was continued in seventeenth-century French formal gardens.

Medieval Italian gardens were confined within walls or in cloisters, but in the fifteenth century they became open and outward-looking. The garden at the Villa Medici at Fiesole, near Florence, was one of the first of this new style. On the advice of scholar and architect Leon Battista Alberti, it was built on an elevated site and boasts two major terraces. Constructed out of the hillside – a substantial feat at the time – they provide panoramic views of Florence and the valley of the river Arno.

At the beginning of the seventeenth century in France, the vast landscaped grounds demanded by Louis XIII and Cardinal Richelieu

Above: In this vista, framed by the sculptural entrance, the eye is led by an avenue of trees to the fifteenth-century Villa Medici on the crest of a densely wooded hill. The implication of such a layout is that the villa, located near Florence, Italy, commands all the landscape below it.

Opposite: The Villa Medici was one of the first to take advantage of an elevated position for its garden design. Stepped terraces are cut into the steep hillside, allowing the landscape below to be admired as part of the garden.

This engraving of the garden at Versailles clearly shows the intention of its designer André Le Nôtre. Beyond the ornamental pool, the lines of the Grand Canal converge at a point on the horizon and give the impression that the garden goes on to infinity.

meant that the idea that symmetry implied a perceptible boundary could no longer apply. Instead, symmetry was replaced by a system in which the garden was balanced around a main axis, with the possibility, in theory, of the garden extending to infinity. Long formal vistas were designed to give the impression that gardens were endless.

An example of this type of design is the garden developed by Louis XIV at Versailles, the scale and magnificence of which became the envy of Europe. It was begun in 1662 and designed by André Le Nôtre who used the points of the compass to establish the garden's main axes, identified by the cruciform shape of the Grand Canal.

The garden features a long perspective, or *à perte de vue*, along its east–west axis. Below the west-facing façade of the palace's *Grande*

Galerie, Le Nôtre introduced a *parterre d'eau*, consisting mainly of two vast sheets of water, called mirrors, that produce a sense of infinite space. From the palace, the eye is led by the "mirrors", through a tree-lined avenue, down a long lawn, to the Grand Canal, which on a summer's evening seems to vanish into the haze of the setting sun.

In the eighteenth century the concept of gardens without boundaries was most fully expressed in Europe by the emergent English Landscape Movement. Followers adopted the ha-ha, which had been invented by French designers of formal gardens to conceal the boundary between garden and surroundings, using it in their more natural style of garden design. At the beginning of eighteenth century, the politician and philosopher Anthony Ashley Cooper (Third Earl of Shaftsbury) had written that the Renaissance designers had put architecture and garden structures before plants and that he could no longer "resist the passion for things of a natural kind". His view was supported by the poet and essayist Joseph Addison who wrote in *The Spectator* that "we must honour nature rather than deviate from it", recommending that all elements of formality be replaced by irregularity.

Two professional gardeners, Stephen Switzer and Charles Bridgeman, were among the first to promote this more liberal approach to design.

This ha-ha at Clinton Lodge, Sussex, shows how such devices were traditionally constructed. The trimmed lawn of the house terminates at a retaining wall, with its buttresses clearly visible. The other side of the ha-ha is formed by a gentle grassy slope, which merges into the adjoining pasture.

Left: This mossy landscape is part of the garden of the Imperial Palace in Kyoto, Japan. This scene is one of number of specially designed views created along a path. Described as a "stroll" or "tour" garden, it is intended to be experienced as a series of individual scenes rather than as a single whole.

Right: A serpentine rill leads through a still pool, known as the Cold Bath, and into a gloomy woodland glade in this garden at Rousham House in Oxfordshire. Created by William Kent in the 1730s, it is one of the finest examples of the picturesque style of landscape design.

Switzer's early suggestions were that "all the adjacent country [should] be laid open to view", and that gardens should no longer be enclosed with walls "by which the eye is as it were imprisoned and the feet fettered in the midst of the extensive charms of nature."

These opinions probably influenced Bridgeman, who in 1715 introduced the masterstroke that led to all that followed – the ha-ha, first used in Britain on an extensive scale at Stowe, in Buckinghamshire. The original drawings for Stowe, dating from 1720, reveal the important part that this feature was to play in the development of the landscape garden. The ground of the park beyond the sunken fence was, according to the then-contemporary commentator Horace Walpole, "harmonized with the lawn within and the garden in its turn was set free from its prim regularity, that it might assort with the wilder country without."

Lancelot "Capability" Brown (1715–83) used the device as a means of creating an invisible livestock barrier, that would not interrupt a favoured view. Brown allowed his park-like gardens to lap up to the house as

In this view over a wild flower meadow and woodland it is difficult to distinguish where the garden ends and the adjoining natural landscape begins. This picturesque scene was created by Humphrey Repton at Endsleigh in Devon.

well as to extend outwards to connect with the landscape outside the property's boundary. He dominated landscape design from 1751, and in the essay "Modern Gardening" (1780) Horace Walpole included a tribute to Brown: "How rich, how gay, how picturesque the face of the country…the demolition of walls laying open each improvement."

In the design of their gardens Brown and his contemporaries sought wherever possible to borrow distant landscapes or views and make them part of each garden's design. It was a practice also employed by the creators of traditional Japanese gardens, but they did not rely on devices such as the ha-ha. *Shakkei*, the Japanese word for borrowed landscape, refers to the way in which external views are captured and made integral parts of a garden by careful positioning of the planting, and by making use of the natural contours of the garden landscape.

Traditional Japanese gardens are influenced by Shintoism or Buddhism, which regard nature as sacred, and by the fact that in Japan space is at a premium. There are essentially two types of traditional Japanese garden: one is intended and designed for contemplation and is best represented by the symbolic Zen "dry" gardens; the other is the "tour" or "stroll" garden, to be walked and experienced as a sequence of different views. Many exterior gardens of the Edo Period (1603–1867) were conceived as tour gardens to create the illusion that the area they covered was bigger than in reality. This was achieved by a combination of concealment and carefully selected views, which revealed some but not all of the site.

The tour garden of the Katsura Imperial Palace in Kyoto – also referred to as Rikyu, or Detached Palace – is a fine example of this type of garden. Begun in 1620, it is surrounded by trees and looks in upon itself as a series of views presented along a path that leads around a central lake. Views of miniature mountains, pebbled shores, and islands are revealed along a path of some 1,760 stepping-stones.

The concept of the tour garden also appears in eighteenth-century English gardens, most notably at Rousham House in Oxfordshire. Rousham was designed by William Kent (1674–1748), who had given

Emerging out of a woodland is Fallingwater, the best-known house designed by Frank Lloyd Wright. The concrete and stone house has no garden – instead, Wright adopted a natural rocky waterfall and incorporated it within the building's architecture.

direction to the newly formed English Landscape Movement by his avoidance of regularity and his adoption of a "picturesque" style, inspired by the works of the French artists Claude Lorrain and Nicolas Poussin, whose idealized painted vistas often featured classical antiquities.

Rousham is the only garden designed by Kent that remains as he left it. The garden contains only two straight lines – the rest is an irregular landscape consisting of a series of views. Paths connect vignettes of classical statuary and architectural follies. (During this era, follies were often built on pieces of land outside the confines of the main garden and were intended to add to the impression that the garden extended far beyond its actual boundaries.) The statues in one vignette look towards a fake neo-gothic façade; seen in silhoutte, this "eye-catcher" draws the undulating Oxfordshire countryside into the garden.

In the late eighteenth and early nineteenth centuries Humphry Repton (1752–1818) took up the mantle from Kent and Brown. His 1810 design for Endsleigh in Devon features a grassy terrace that stretches away from the cottage-style house, down a slope and to a wildflower meadow. Informal and natural planting, in the cottage-garden style, was to reappear in the late twentieth century as part of an ecological and environmentally-friendly approach to garden design.

Throughout the twentieth century, the influence of architecture on garden design was substantial. In the early years of the century a new style of architecture emerged that was based on form following function and identified by its clean geometric lines and lack of ornamentation. This modernist style, as it is now called, was promoted by architects such as Walter Gropius and Adolf Loos in Europe, and by Frank Lloyd Wright in the United States. Their new aesthetic ideals presented a challenge to the garden designers of the day not only because these architects had their own ideas on how a house should relate to its environment, but also because landscape design at the time of the emergence of this new style of architecture was still entrenched in the traditions of previous centuries.

Frank Lloyd Wright's famous Fallingwater, designed for Edgar J. Kaufmann, Sr. at Bear Run, Pennsylvania in 1937, was not created by a garden designer. The house is set into the wild landscape, with no terrace or conventional garden to act as a transition. Stone, quarried nearby, forms massive piers, from which huge, cantilevered reinforced-

Opposite: **Designed by Le Corbusier, Villa Savoye, at Poissy-sur-Seine, sits in a field and no attempt has been made to landscape the site or develop it as a garden. Le Corbusier was adamant that the field should remain as found, preferring instead to incorporate a garden terrace as an outdoor room on the roof of the building.**

This steel-and-glass house belonged to its architect Charles Eames. Aware of the visual effect on the natural surroundings, the architect concealed it behind trees. He left the remaining part of the site to nature, rather than intrude any further into the property's beautiful meadow landscape.

concrete slabs, that project housing the living spaces project over rocky outcrops and the cascading river. At Fallingwater the landscape is more adopted than borrowed in that the surrounding untouched woodland is the garden. This idea of a garden by adoption is one that has been taken on board by several garden designers in recent years.

A respect for the landscape also influenced the American architect Charles Eames when he came to design his own home at Pacific Palisades, California, in 1949. The building is essentially formed of two boxes, with each wall plane a geometric composition of rectangular windows and coloured panels, in a style reminiscent of the abstract paintings of the Dutch artist Piet Mondrian. Rather than interfere with this wild site, Eames placed the house deep in the steep hillside, behind the shelter of giant eucalyptus trees. He chose to leave uncultivated the wooded landscape around the house – the garden is simply the existing meadow, restored where necessary with rye grass and wildflowers.

One of the most radical ideas concerning the relationship between a house and its landscape is expressed in the French architect Le Corbusier's 1930 design for the Villa Savoye, at Poissy-sur-Seine, France. Here, Le Corbusier has raised the indoor and outdoor living accommodation up off the ground. The architect, who believed in clarity of design, felt that a garden or terrace at ground level would serve to confuse the distinction between man-made and natural forms. At Villa Savoye the unaffected surrounding landscape is not only allowed to come up to the house but also to continue under it.

By the 1930s some landscape architects, particularly in the United States, had become aware of the need to find a modern language for landscape design and a style that reflected the spirit of the new architecture. One such architect was Thomas Church. Along with Dan Kiley and James Rose, Church had come into contact with the architect Walter Gropius. Responding to Gropius's rational design aesthetics, Church developed a strategy that was not based on applying old

In Thomas Church's El Novillero garden at the north end of San Francisco Bay, California, the kidney-shaped swimming pool reflects the curving lines of the distant landscape. This biomorphic pool was revolutionary in its day, and transformed the design of swimming pools.

forms to new situations but, instead, on allowing the "problem" to generate the solution.

Church evolved what is now described as "Californian style" as a way of dealing with hillside sites. With wooden decks and raised planting beds, his gardens were designed for leisure and low-maintenance. Church also related his gardens to the surrounding landscape in a modern way, most notably in his 1949 design for the El Novillero garden at Sonoma, California. Here, he introduced organic shapes in the swimming pool and the edges of the paving to echo the rolling hills and salt marshes of the valley beyond.

At about the same time, the Brazilian landscape architect Roberto Burle Marx developed a personal style, that was essentially Brazilian and also very modern. Burle Marx was eager to create garden designs based on native plants and he was also influenced by his attraction to the paintings of the surrealist Joan Miró. His subsequent garden designs vary in appearance but in essence consist of native plants arranged in sculptural groups within free-flowing painterly patterns of colourful ground-cover and paths. His informal style allows his gardens to blend seamlessly with the existing, surrounding natural landscape.

Recent developments in architectural engineering have allowed houses to have very different relationships with their gardens. Designed by Future Systems, the Pod House, which is sited on a coastal cliff top in Pembrokeshire, Wales, is one such building. Built in the 1990s the underground house is virtually invisible, apart from its glass front. The earth that was removed during its construction was restored over the top to provide a garden that is indistinguishable from the surrounding landscape. Such a relationship between a house and garden raises questions regarding the definition of a garden. At the Pod House, it is simply the original landscape left as found.

The world of art has also contributed to the argument of what constitutes a garden. Since the 1960s many artists have chosen to create works that are made with or within the landscape. Sculptors have

Designed by the American landscape architect Richard Haag, this landscape at the Bloedel Reserve, Seattle, reveals the close association between land art and garden design. The turf and planted mounds are strongly sculptural yet, collectively, they suggest a Japanese-inspired garden.

Previous pages: The Monteiro Garden near Rio de Janeiro, Brazil, was designed by Burle Marx. Here, the influence of the English park-style landscape is modified by Burle Marx's use of indigenous trees or shrubs, and by eye-catching, strong-coloured, ground-cover foliage.

Left: Looking like something out of sci-fi, the Pod House designed by Future Systems peers out from beneath the ground in cliffs above the Pembrokeshire coast. It is a house designed to respect the landscape that it belongs to, and its "garden" is the unspoilt natural surroundings.

Above right: Truncated telegraph poles feature in a sculptural landscape designed by George Hargreaves at Byxbee Park. The avenue of poles leads the eye towards a recess in an earthwork (also part of the scheme) which was intended to transform a landfill site into a public park.

attacked the landscape on vast scale. In 1970, the American artist Robert Smithson created a 5,000-m (16,400-ft) long "Spiral Jetty" in the Great Salt Lake, and in 1977 Walter De Maria inserted in the ground a regular grid of 400 stainless steel rods, each 6m (20ft) high, in an area of New Mexico prone to regular and violent thunderstorms.

This "land" or "environmental" art movement was stimulated by many factors, one being the "flower power" philosophy that emerged during the second half of the 1960s. Its followers desired a closer relationship with the natural world, which they assumed was the way of earlier civilizations. Many artists, sympathetic to these ideas, were keen to cast off the pressures of the commercial art world and to relocate and work in remote locations. For these artists, land art meant a rejection of studio-based object-making in favour of an art form that was at one with the landscape rather than imposed upon it. Part of the appeal of this kind of art was that it often had only a short lifespan.

Following this lead, many landscape architects have chosen to work in a similar vein. The American George Hargreaves, for example, combined land art and landscape design in his scheme for Byxbee Park in Palo Alto, California. Completed in 1992, it represents a break from the old tradition of park design that relied upon eighteenth-century English landscape formulae. Hargreaves' unorthodox solution for this derelict landfill site includes expanses of native grasses, earth-forms, highway barriers, and truncated telegraph poles, which are intended to extend the park visually into the surrounding landscape. These cross-over artists have introduced the concept of landscape design as an "idea", rather than a response to functional necessity.

The resulting "new" landscapes challenge the traditional definition of a garden and extend its boundaries both conceptually and visually.

The Borrowed Landscape

Above right: At Gainesway Farm in Lexington, KY, the American landscape architect A.E. Bye has employed an ornamental canal set within an avenue of established oak trees to create a sense of depth and to lead the eye to the horizon.

Left: Bye installed a serpentine stone wall at Gainesway Farm in order to separate the garden landscape from the pasture land. As the wall sweeps up from the river it changes from a free-standing structure into a ha-ha to allow an uninterrupted view of the lake and wooded hills.

The concept of the "borrowed landscape", or "borrowed view", has been used in the design of gardens since ancient times. The earliest examples can be traced back to ancient China and Japan, where the aim was to make small gardens seem bigger. The term refers to the way a distant landscape is drawn into the garden to enhance it and extend its parameters. In many cases, the barrier that usually marks the property's boundary is avoided or concealed to emphasize a view, and to permit an apparently seamless transition from the garden to the land beyond.

A borrowed view is attained most easily if the house and garden are in an elevated position. Many fifteenth-century Italian villas were built in such locations, with the hills of Tuscany providing an ideal setting. However by the seventeenth century other methods had been devised to allow a garden to borrow a view. Architectural features were developed to conceal boundaries and incorporate the distant landscape into the garden's design. The best known of these is the ha-ha.

A ha-ha is a dry ditch formed by a retaining wall on the garden side and a gentle slope on the other. It is invisible from the house, making the garden seem to flow into the landscape. The ha-ha first was first introduced in the seventeenth century in formal gardens such as those at Versailles, France. It was adopted by the English Landscape Movement in the eighteenth century and was popularly used to satisfy the ambitions of the new land-owning classes because its effect is to make a property seem more extensive. The ha-ha is still used today, although often serving new functions and evolving into new forms.

In 1983 the American landscape architect A.E. Bye incorporated a ha-ha into his design for the garden of Gainesway Farm, a barn

Mysterious figure-like forms are seen in silhouette through a living gothic archway in the woodland part of the Duncan's garden at Kerscott in Devon. The contrast between the dark foreground and the illuminated area beyond the arch creates a heightened sense of depth.

conversion at Lexington in Kentucky. Bye is respected as a designer who works in sympathy and harmony with the natural landscape. Each of his garden designs is unique because it is a direct response to the *genius loci* and the regional idiosyncrasies or characteristics of the natural landscape in which he is working.

The Gainesway house is situated near a group of mature oak trees within a 200-ha (500-acre) farm. The clients required an outdoor sitting-and-entertaining area near the house, and insisted that it should have views of the farm estate, its river and man-made lake, as well as the hills beyond. The main feature of Bye's solution is the ha-ha: sited to the east of the residence, the 137-m (450-ft) long ha-ha was introduced to replace a visually intrusive horse-fence, which also obstructed the view down to the river and lake. The device links the garden with the more distant landscape of rolling hills and tree lines, and its meandering curved line was, according to Bye, "profiled to echo the clean rises and falls of the surrounding fields … and the edge of a lake across the valley." The ha-ha follows the natural contours of the meadow as it drops towards the river. The wall, a true ha-ha along most of its length, emerges to stand above ground level as the land falls away. By clever positioning and shifting earth, Bye has made the wall invisible from the house and its immediate garden. Constructed from local stone, it sits comfortably in its rural setting.

A ha-ha can be expensive, since it requires the excavation of trenches and the building of retaining walls. At Kerscott, the Devon home of Jessica and Peter Duncan, a fence serves as a boundary in the family garden. A fence usually forms a distinct barrier between a garden and the land beyond, but at Kerscott it has been designed to do the opposite.

Framed by the trunks and canopies of nearby trees, the view of a distant rounded hill is enhanced by the way in which Jessica Duncan has shaped the dogwood and willow "fence" at Kerscott. By imitating the hill's form, Duncan draws the Devon landscape into the garden.

Jessica Duncan, the garden's designer, felt it was essential that the garden should have views of the beautiful surrounding countryside. To give the garden protection from the prevailing wind, a perimeter screen of shrubs and trees was planted. However, the planting was not too dense since it was important to retain glimpses of the external landscape, which Jessica wanted to become part of the garden's design.

A fence was also needed to keep out livestock belonging to the adjoining farm. The resultant barrier is, in fact, more of a hedge: it is a "living fence" grown from dogwood and reinforced with willow twigs. Its profile is trimmed in a curve to mirror the distinctive shape of a hill about a mile away, and the interwoven willow also mimics this distant land form. Although the fence clearly acts both as a boundary and a barrier, its clever shape draws the natural features of the surrounding Devon landscape into the garden.

American landscape architect Steve Martino prefers to use architectural structures when borrowing a view. For a small garden near Phoenix, Arizona, he has developed the basic principle of the ha-ha, disguising it as a swimming pool. Located on one side of a small canyon, the slightly elevated property has a clear view of the semi-desert hills on the other side. "Swimming pools are used only one percent of the day,"

Opposite: A swimming pool forms the boundary of this garden in Phoenix, designed by Steve Martino. The water avoids the need for a wall or balustrade, allowing a clear view of the desert hills; it also both reflects the sky and the immediate surroundings.

Below: In this Connecticut garden designed by Dan Kiley, a canal forms the edge of a raised lawn. The water acts as a ha-ha, emphasizing the view – a series of horizontal lines that begin at the lawn and end at the distant lake and hills.

Below: **At the DeBartolo residence in Paradise Valley, the lawn terrace is overlaid with narrow concrete strips in a grid pattern that connects with a series of freestanding walls. Designer Steve Martino has used these walls as picture frames to capture views of the desert.**

claims Martino. "Ninety-nine percent of the time they're just visual." Here, the pool is used to provide a connection between the small garden and the wider landscape beyond.

The retaining wall on the far side of the pool has a narrow edge and acts like a small ha-ha, providing an uninterrupted view of the distant hills, which are also reflected in the water. Beyond the pool, a security fence is cleverly designed not to interfere with the outlook. Wire-mesh screens are supported on steel supports, which are shaped like agave leaves and project outwards at right angles. The statuesque black-painted shapes contrast strongly with the pale background of the surrounding landscape, and render the light mesh fence almost invisible.

Martino has earned a reputation for his pioneering work with native plants, particularly those associated with the desert regions of the United States. His knowledge has enabled him to create gardens that are in keeping with their natural surroundings, but he regards plants as "incidental to the garden's design". As far as he is concerned, the architectural aspect, or "hard-landscaping", is more important in the garden than the plants, stating "It is walls that really define the space."

The design potential of freestanding walls is apparent in Paradise Valley, Arizona, in a garden that Martino created for Jack and Pat DeBartolo Jr. The clients wanted him to integrate their minimalist one-room house into its mountainous desert environment. Martino has achieved this by use of walls as well as through his choice of planting material, which is based on the flora and vegetation indigenous to this high desert region. It is the walls, however, that enable the garden to borrow the view of the desert landscape.

The east-facing side of the site slopes down, away from the front of the house. This direction affords the best views, so a lawn terrace was established level with the house. On the south side of the terrace is a tall

Left: The DeBartolo house is accessed from the road via steps located to the side of the main lawn terrace. As the steps rise upwards, they pass through a series of smaller terraces. In the lower terraces, and on the remaining exposed slope, Martino has installed informal natural-looking planting.

screening wall, constructed to provide shade for a small swimming pool, also located on this level. Below the terrace on the remaining exposed slope, Martino has introduced informal planting.

The lawn terrace acts as a transition between the simple rigid architecture of the house and the natural forms of the desert landscape. The terrace's retaining wall functions like a ha-ha and is invisible from the house and lawn. A series of freestanding white walls are positioned at right angles above this retaining wall, forming a colonnade that echoes the house architecture; and the space between each wall serves as a picture window to frame the mountain scenery beyond.

The position of the house, its formal garden, and its open views represents a revival of Renaissance ideas and is reminiscent of a traditional fifteenth-century Italian villa. In 1452, in his treatise *De Re Edificatoria*, the Italian Renaissance architect and scholar Leon Battista Alberti suggested that the house and garden should be treated as an integrated whole, and that the garden should no longer be an enclosed space but should be wedded to the landscape. His ideas led to villas

Opposite: The surroundings of this house, designed by architect Rick Joy, have not been turned into a garden, and the sparse vegetation of the semi-desert landscape has been left untouched. Instead, a courtyard and covered enclosure provides the outdoor living space.

Below: Built in an elevated position, the terrace and pool of the Rick Joy house borrow spectacular views of the desert terrain of southern Arizona. A window-like opening in the outdoor room frames the scenery so it becomes like a painting on a wall.

being built in elevated positions with terraced gardens that afforded uninterrupted views of the surrounding countryside.

The Italian villa was the inspiration for the design of many of the early formal gardens in the United States. During the "Country Place" era, between the 1880s and 1920s, American entrepreneurs spent vast, virtually untaxed fortunes on commissioning large country homes with grand gardens to match. The Wall Street Crash in 1929 ended this boom period, but economic revival in the second half of the twentieth century, coupled with an abundance of inexpensive space (mainly in more remote and climatically harsher regions), prompted another surge in the building of private residences and a proliferation of "new" landscapes. Dan Kiley created one such landscape for a new house in rural Connecticut.

Born in 1912, Kiley was one of a new generation of landscape architects that included James Rose, Garrett Eckbo, and Thomas Church. He trained at Harvard University's Graduate School of Design and was part of a movement that favoured a modern approach to landscape design. At Harvard he came into contact with the former director of the Bauhaus school of architecture in Germany, Water Gropius. While at the Bauhaus, Gropius had introduced a new architectural aesthetic, one that was based on standardization and rationalism, with form dictated by function. Kiley and his contemporaries were eager to develop new landscapes and gardens to complement this modernist architecture.

Kiley's landscapes were based on a desire to find functional solutions to a stated design problem. In his own words, "Landscape is not mere adornment but an integral part of the deposition of space, plane line and structure with which it is associated." Like the creators of the French formal gardens he also believed that the man-made landscape

Above: Dry-stone sculptures punctuate the landscape, providing interest in a "garden" that is no more than a clearing in a heavily wooded area. The sculptures belongs to a house designed by the Australian architect Harry Seidler and is located at the top of an escarpment in the Southern Highlands of New South Wales, Australia.

Right: Seidler's house has no need a garden. It flies out from the rugged terrain of the cliff top, allowing its owners to enjoy a much larger landscape.

should provide an obvious contrast to the natural world – an approach that is evident in his design for the garden of the Connecticut house.

The Connecticut project was begun in 1995, on a site is over 240ha (593 acres) of undulating New England farmland. The new house was built over the foundations of the original farmstead, and the principal formal gardens were to be established on the west-facing side of the house, where the land sloped downwards. Kiley's brief was to integrate the house with the garden, to establish usable, level recreation areas, and to make the most of the magnificent view of the Taconic Hills and the wonderful sunsets.

The overall scheme is a strong geometric plan of interconnecting spaces, including formal lawns and terraces. Introduced into these are

These groups of large-growing willow and eucalyptus trees make it hard to see that this garden, created by designer Fiona Naylor, is on a roof. The trees hide the railings, and thus the garden's boundary, but they still allow a glimpse of the buildings beyond. This makes the garden space seem to extend outwards and avoids any sense of confinement.

lines of trees, squares of four trees, and pairs of trees in circles. A rectangular lawn, large enough for croquet, was established at the northwest corner of the house. To achieve this level surface on the sloping site required two substantial retaining walls, but Kiley cleverly disguised them as canals, each one 30m (100ft) long. The canals border the lawn, and act as ha-has, negating the need for an intrusive balustrade, which would interrupt the view of the landscape beyond.

The surface of each canal is level with the lawn, with only a narrow strip of black slate separating the two, and the water is allowed to flow over the canals' outer bank, creating what is called an "infinity edge". Below the edge, the water drops into a narrow gully, which leads to a square fountain pool at the lawn's outermost corner. The canals and fountain pool are lined with black-slate tiles to heighten the mirror-like quality of the water and enable it to reflect both the sky and the surrounding hills. Only at gully level is the significant concrete retaining wall evident – from the house and its attached shady pergola and terraced garden, all that is visible is the glass-like rim of water, with uninterrupted views of the New England landscape beyond.

In Italian Renaissance villas the hillside architecture and outward-looking terraces that married the gardens to the surrounding environment. This fifteenth-century method of borrowing an external landscape was brought into the twenty-first century in a house designed by American architect Rick Joy.

The house is in southern Arizona, near to the Mexican border. Renowned for its spectacular lightning storms, this semi-desert region is dramatic and awesome. The clients love the landscape and wanted a house that would embrace it. The resulting single-storey building of rusted steel and glass is positioned on an elevated platform, which is cut into a slight natural slope. The sparsely vegetated desert floor drops away, providing the house with breathtaking views of distant snow-capped mountains which form a jagged horizon to a vast expanse of sky.

The garden is essentially a courtyard. A group of mesquite trees provides shade, and there is additional fragrant planting in raised beds. Planters, precise concrete paving, and rectilinear pools reflect the formal, modernist style of the house. At the western end of the courtyard, a swimming pool forms the only barrier between the house and distant horizon. Interior and exterior spaces link with each other, and covered enclosures have window-like openings that frame a series of chosen vistas.

Alberti's idea that a house should be built in an elevated position to maximize views was taken to extremes by the architect Harry Seidler in

Even a tiny balcony can be designed to borrow a view. In this case, designer Robin Cameron Don has used plants with large leaves to blur the edges of the small space and connect it with planting in adjacent gardens.

A sculpture of a lion sits at the point where the terrace wall gives way to a pool, forming a spectacular edge to the terrace of this garden in Argentina, designed by landscape architect Juan Grimm. The pool terrace, bathed in the evening sun, provides the residents with uninterrupted views of the landscape below and beyond.

his design for a house in the Southern Highlands of New South Wales, Australia. Located on the crest of a high, rocky escarpment, the holiday home projects perilously over a sheer cliff-face that drops steeply to a river far below.

The house is essentially L-shaped in plan. The longer leg of the "L", which contains the main living and dining areas, points westwards over the cliff, supported by a cantilevered steel framework that holds this part of the house clear of the rocky terrain. All the walls of this section are glazed from floor to ceiling, and on the north side, sliding panels give access to an open deck, which continues beyond the living accommodation to become a spectacular viewing platform.

The house is situated in the midst of a wilderness. The surrounding landscape has been left untouched where possible, with some reshaping undertaken only to provide access. Walls extend south beyond the house as a retaining element to provide a level entrance and garage area, and northwards as a protecting screen for the swimming pool, which is installed within the natural contours of the rocky landscape.

The local red sandstone is used for the random-built retaining walls, and paths are kept as informal as possible. The house is intended as a retreat, and the garden is no more than a practical modification of the natural surroundings. The real "garden" of this property is the landscape of the Southern Highlands, which the house flies out over.

An elevated position does not always provide beautiful views; for example, a roof garden in an urban environment. However, the lofty position of such a garden can still be exploited to create a feeling of space. A roof terrace designed by Fiona Naylor for a London apartment has a backdrop of tall buildings and rooftops. Despite the obvious need for a secure and substantial railing, she has managed both to blur this boundary and to establish a sense of disbelief about the true location

Designer Bonita Bulaitis took advantage of the steep slope of this front garden in Fowey, Cornwall, to create a twin-level water feature. The water drops from a large pool on the upper terrace into a reservoir in the lower, more sheltered sitting area.

of the garden; it is hard to imagine that the site is high up among the rooftops of a major city.

Planting in containers around the perimeter of the roof terrace conceals the railings but retains a glimpse of what lies beyond, allowing the gap between the terrace and the buildings on the far side of the street to become part of the garden space. The buildings appear to form the garden's boundary, thus enlarging the rooftop space. The increased sense of space is reinforced by Naylor's choice of plants, which includes large-growing bamboos, as well as willow and eucalyptus – trees not normally associated with a rooftop site. The hard-landscape ingredients are also more likely to be found in gardens on the ground than on rooftop ones. Apart from a wooden deck, the floor is covered in gravel and cobblestones, and the garden also boasts a water rill.

Designer Robin Cameron Don has created a similar effect in his scheme for a balcony garden in London. The small space is packed with large-growing foliage plants, including tree ferns. The container-grown plants partially hide the walls and balustrade, and, from the rear of the balcony, the foliage merges with plants in the nearby garden. As with the Naylor's roof terrace, the verdure of the balcony contradicts its small size and urban location.

When a view includes a seascape or a river estuary, a water feature is an ideal way of relating the garden to its surroundings. In such a situation the infinity-edge pool is a popular solution. Like the ha-ha, it

Opposite: Stacks of local stone and slate add sculptural interest in the upper terrace of the garden at Fowey. Bulaitis has employed the reflective surface of the upper pool as a means of merging the garden with the distant landscape of hills and the river estuary.

Above right: At Stone Meadow, Chilmark, Mass., the American architect Stephen Stimson introduced narrow stone bands, like steps, into the gentle slope. They are tied into the plinth wall of the main lawn and with it they echo the horizontal character of the coastal landscape.

Left: At this Cape Cod residence Stephen Stimson's use of an "infinity edge" pool is particularly appropriate. The watery plane of the swimming pool serves to connect the garden visually to its context, a seascape of tidal pools, ocean and sky.

removes the need for a wall or fence, but is dependent on the garden being in an elevated position for uninterrupted views of the adjacent terrain. Canals served this purpose in Dan Kiley's Connecticut garden, while landscape architect Steve Martino used a swimming pool to create an infinity edge in his Phoenix garden. Ornamental pools can be exploited to create such a device, which is even more effective in a seascape.

An infinity-edge pool in a modest-sized garden at Fowey in Cornwall is used to connect the garden visually with its immediate environment of river estuary, town, and hills. The site is the front garden of a three-storey, mid-terrace property. The challenge that faced the British designer, Bonita Bulaitis, was that, as well as needing to be an outdoor recreational area, the garden also had to remain the main access to the house. Another problem is the site's steep slope: it drops 6m (20ft) from the front door to the road below. Whatever the solution, both client and designer agreed that it was essential to retain a view of the Fowey estuary.

Bulaitis's design divides the sloping site into two main terraces, with two stepped areas, located towards the foot of the garden, and dedicated to planting. She left the garden steps as they were, retaining the most direct route to the front door. The lower of the two terraces is a sitting-cum-dining area, which is sheltered on either side by the garden's boundary walls. Despite being open to the front, the space feels enclosed, as Bulaitis has exploited the neighbouring properties and roof lines of houses below to provide a sense of seclusion.

From the upper terrace the outlook is impressive and imposing, reflecting how Bulaitis opted to work with Fowey's dramatic setting. At the far edge of the terrace, she incorporated an ornamental infinity-edge pool. The surface of this rectangular piece of water makes a visual link

Designed by Pietro Porcini, this decorative walled garden at Cetona, near Rome, borrows a view from the facing woodland. The wall is rendered almost invisible by being smothered in foliage and flowers, and this allows the terraced garden to merge with the distant vegetation.

with the waters of the river, and also reflects the sky and hills beyond. On wet days, not unusual in this part of Britain, the grey-blue slate paving of the upper terrace seems to dissolve into the grey waters of the pool and estuary below. Bulaitis's design methodology for the garden at Fowey is essentially an intuitive one, inspired by a great sense of place and held together by a strong formal composition.

The "infinity edge" pool is a popular garden feature in warmer climes, where outdoor swimming pools and ornamental pools provide refreshing focal points. When the garden is located in an elevated position the juxtaposition of water and distant landscape can be particularly effective, as illustrated by a garden designed by the Argentine landscape architect Juan Grimm. Situated in central Argentina, the garden affords spectacular views across a fertile valley to high mountains. In one corner of a lawn terrace Grimm has set a six-sided pool, surrounded by a paved walkway and sitting area. A low wall terminates at the furthermost side of the pool, where the water slips over an invisible edge into a lower reservoir. The sound of falling water is welcome but it is the pool's infinity edge that is the real treat as it opens the garden to the distant landcape, and emphasizes the view. Planting is kept discreet, and nothing is allowed to distract from the garden viewpoint, which is to the mountainous landscape beyond.

In garden designer Jinny Blooms' own garden a pathway leads through a richly planted herbaceous border that seems to extend without restriction into the distance. The sense of continuity is created not by architectural devices but by the thoughtful positioning of the planting.

A similar approach can be found in the work of the American landscape architect Stephen Stimson. He studied at the Harvard Graduate School of Design, and was influenced by the formal, minimalist landscapes of Dan Kiley. Stimson's childhood was spent on a farm in Massachusetts, and this rural upbringing instilled in him an awareness of the natural and agricultural landscape. He frequently employs the elements of a surrounding landscape to integrate his formal-style gardens with the immediate environment, both visually and ecologically. The boundary between "wild" and "cultivated" is interconnected by the use of features such as ha-has, walkways, and, most notably, pools.

When water within a garden is used to "borrow" a natural water-land or seascape the effect can be stunning, as Stimson's design for a house in coastal Massachusetts demonstrates. The property sits in an elavated position on Cape Cod's southern shoreline. On the seaward side of the residence natural stone walls retain a multi-level terrace and a rectangular swimming pool that projects outward towards the sea. The pool not only has a recreational function but connects the landscape of the garden with its seascape environment. It is bordered along its far corner by an "infinity edge", which creates an apparently edgeless surface of water that merges with the nearby tidal marshes and ocean.

A wooden pier, complete with railings and scattered blocks of timber, creates a nautical feeling that relates this garden, designed by Susan Campbell, to its coastal setting. Beyond the deck are the waters of the Solent and, on the horizon the Isle of Wight, off the south coast of England.

The swimming pool is set within a floor of blue/grey paving. water from a circular spa flows into the pool via a narrow channel that zigzags across the pool terrace to make a further visual reference to the coastal landscape. The channel's angular meander echoes the mosquito ditches cut into the estuary marshes as well as the natural inlets of the shoreline.

Stimson employed a different approach when he sought to integrate another coastal property, known as Stone Meadow, with its surroundings at Chilmark, also in Massachusetts. He took the features of the natural environment – the wild meadows and the local geography, as well as the vast ocean view – and organized them into a simple composition of space and levels.

The south façade of the house rises up from a plinth-like lawn, established by using a stone retaining wall on the gently sloping ground. This grass platform extends outwards towards a low, uncultivated meadow. The top of the far retaining wall is at the same level as the lawn, and its stone coping forms a distinct line that runs parallel with the distant horizon. The wall, which acts like a ha-ha, separates the formal garden from the areas that Stimson has left to nature and, at the same time, invites the eye outwards, towards the sea.

Steps cut into the garden wall lead down from the lawn to join with paths that lead through the meadow of grasses and sedges into the larger untouched landscape. To the west side of the raised lawn, narrow stone bands, which act as risers for a series of stepped, sloping grass terraces, provide further horizontal lines. These lawn "steps" conclude in a mown edge, where they meet the longer meadow grass. At Stone Meadow Stimson "borrows" the natural wild meadows as well as the ocean view. Not all the garden at Stone Meadow is exposed to the elements. To the north-east of the house, and concealed between a protective hedgerow of black locust and a red cedar, is a secluded garden containing a swimming pool and tennis court.

Planting to disguise a wall or unwanted fence can be a means of enabling a garden to borrow a view. In Cetona, near Rome, is a garden in which Italian designer Pietro Porcini demonstrates how a wall need not be a visual obstruction. In his scheme, the tall, brick wall enclosing a courtyard is clothed in vegetation, making it lose its finite edge, and blend with the planting outside, where the garden rises as woodland.

Other sites have required a more unorthodox approach. Susan Campbell provides a novel solution in her design for a garden in Hampshire. The garden backs on to the Solent, a strait of the English Channel that separates the mainland coast from the Isle of Wight. Where

Mist hovers over this circular pool set in a garden on the western shore of Chesapeake Bay, created by Wolfgang Oehme and James van Sweden. This and other features are deliberately simple to ensure that the garden's beautiful surroundings are not challenged.

In their design for this garden that faces on to Chesapeake Bay, landscape designers Oehme and van Sweden have introduced broad masses of low planting to make a visual reference to the distant horizon line. Here, the oak, one of several in the garden, serves as a solitary vertical.

the garden meets the sea, Campbell has introduced a pier-like, timber structure with nautical details including timber blocks, which resemble mooring posts, and a rope railing with access down to the water. The structure suggests a landing stage or harbour and connects the garden landscape directly to the seascape. By making a visual reference to the area's traditional marine activity, Campbell relates the garden to the social aspects of this seascape, borrowing the view both literally and figuratively.

A more subtle form of borrowing is adopted for a sea-level site on the western shore of Chesapeake Bay. The property is surrounded by an existing, beautiful natural landscape and the garden's designers, Wolfgang Oehme and James van Sweden, felt that this environment should be worked with rather than imposed upon.

The house is a renovated clapboard building, and the garden had several mature oak trees, which needed to be retained. The client's brief also required the inclusion of a swimming pool. Such man-made pools can often look out of place in a natural setting, but the designers did not attempt to disguise theirs, instead relying on restraint and opting for a plain rectangular pool, set within a substantial area of decking. The pool was located between the house and the sea, within an existing lawn, and its simple design and immediate landscape avoid conflict with the expansive seascape surrounding it. The horizontal lines of the decking boards and pool echo both the lines where the lawn meets the sea and those where the sea meets the horizon. The oaks, left untouched, frame and emphasize the view of the bay, which becomes the focus of the garden.

Where new planting has been introduced, it compliments the natural setting. It does not imitate nature and not all the plants included are indigenous. Instead its scale and method allows the garden to be in harmony with its surroundings. The style is unfussy and consists mainly of large groups of a single species. The choice of plant material is important; for example, broad sweeps of ornamental grasses feature strongly. When the sea winds blow, these grasses sway in waves, imitating the water of the nearby ocean. Understatement is the key to the design, allowing this garden to merge imperceptibly with Chesapeake Bay beyond.

Deception

Looking at this garden in California, designed by John L. Wong, the viewer might assume that the lines of paving that define the strip of lawn are parallel. In fact they converge slightly and hence exaggerate the depth of the garden, and draw the eye swiftly to the distant hills.

If the boundaries of a garden are to be rendered invisible, or if a garden landscape is to appear endless, the eye must be fooled. Devices such as the ha-ha does this, as does the infinity-edge pool, but there are methods, that rely on visual deception rather than complex architectural features. Exploiting the optical illusion of perspective is one such method.

The way we see the world about us has long fascinated artists. In their paintings, the ancient Egyptians represented the world in two dimensions, but from multiple angles. The individual elements of the scene were depicted from above or from the side, depending on which view described the item most accurately. A pool might be seen in plan, while the fish swimming in it and the trees surrounding it are shown in elevation. It was not until the Renaissance that a new way of translating the three-dimensional world on to a flat surface evolved. Based on the way our eye actually sees the world about us, this method is called perspective. It assumes a single viewpoint, rather than several, and is most easily explained by looking at the way in which parallel lines seem to converge at the horizon – a hypothetical horizontal line that corresponds to the height of the eye. When placed along these lines, objects of identical size will appear to get smaller the further they are from the eye. Renaissance artists learnt to understand this phenomenon and adopted mathematical systems to replicate it. Unlike the Egyptian method, perspective distorts space and form, but it is now commonly used as a way to depict the world in a natural or realistic manner.

Although perspective is essentially a method by which the three-dimensional world is represented on a two-dimensional surface, an understanding of it has helped landscape designers – from the Renaissance to the present day – to affect the way in which we see a given space. In most cases it is employed to elongate a view and thus, apparently, to extend the visible boundary of a garden. The American

A frosty, misty morning adds a sense of mystery to this garden at The Grove, in Britwell Salome, Oxfordshire. Designed by the late David Hicks, the rectangular pond in the foreground begins a vista that on a clear day extends well beyond the confines of the garden.

landscape architect John L. Wong deliberately distorted perspective in his design for the Nagelberg residence in Ventura County, California. The property has the benefit of an elevated situation, and Wong incorporated an illusion to create the impression that the garden's boundary extends further than it actually does.

The site is essentially triangular, 0.3ha (¾ acre) in size, and located on top of a ridge. The house is a one-storey building consisting of a series of interconnected pavilions, arranged around a courtyard. The intention of the architect, Michael C.F. Chan, was to create the feeling of a hill town. With regard to the landscaping, the clients had requested large lawn areas for recreation, as well as more private enclosed spaces, and most importantly, they wanted the garden to emphasize the views. To the east the house overlooks the fairways of a golf club, beyond which is the natural landscape of the Californian hills.

Wong linked the house with this aspect by exploiting the effects of perspective. Through glass doors that open on to a terrace, the eye is drawn to the distant landscape by two apparently parallel lines of paving. In fact, they are not parallel, but converge slightly as they move away from the house. The normal optical effect that makes lines appear to get closer as they recede into the distance has deliberately been exaggerated, and this fools the eye into interpreting the space as being much longer than it is really is. Planted containers and low lights placed along the strips of paving reinforce the illusion, as does an adjacent avenue of trees.

Whereas Wong has tampered with perspective to alter the way we see things, other garden designers have simply taken advantage of existing visual phenomena. David Hicks, who died in 1999, did this to great effect at his home, The Grove, in Britwell Salome, Oxfordshire.

The Grove is not a garden of flowering plants and borders; instead, the emphasis of the design is on structure and formal composition. One of the most interesting features of Hicks's landscape is the pool garden, which is well hidden, and a surprise when first encountered. The view from the pool garden is also unexpected. Edged with stone coping and cobbles, the large, rectangular stretch of water is surrounded by a screen of clipped chestnuts, except for one opening at the furthermost end. The effect of perspective on the view across the length of the pool towards this opening makes the pool's long parallel sides appear to converge and then connect with a distant avenue of chestnuts. In turn, the avenue leads the eye to an open landscape and a distant obelisk. Placed 0.15km ($\frac{1}{10}$ mile) away, the obelisk serves as a focal point, further extending the view from the pool garden.

This long view is an adaptation of a visual device that dates from French formal gardens of the seventeenth century. At Versailles a stretch of lawn, an avenue of trees, and the water of the Grand Canal, form a long, converging vista that appears to vanish into the distant horizon. At The Grove, the narrow and restricted view produced by the apparently converging lines of pool, hedge, and trees, accentuates distance and creates the illusion of the garden being longer and larger than it is.

A variation of the same principle is to be found in a private garden in Luxembourg. The 0.3-ha ($\frac{3}{4}$-acre) garden was created by its present owners and is made to look much larger, not through the use of a single perspective vista, but by a combination of visual tricks. Water rills and clusters of birch trees function both together and individually, to create a spatially ambiguous garden landscape, the boundary of which is elusive. From one viewpoint, a pair of parallel water rills extend across a lawn

Opposite: **In the foreground of this private garden in Luxembourg, the termination of two water rills is highlighted by the iron rings of a sculpture by the artist Bruno Romeda. In the distance, a group of silver birch trees is silhouetted against a backdrop of firs, which appear to be part of the garden, but are in fact in a field beyond.**

Below: **This informally planted group of silver birches is set within a frequently mowed area of grass. The high canopies reveal the trees' eye-catching white trunks, and these strong vertical forms distract the eye from the garden's boundary.**

towards an informal group of birch trees, and the converging lines of the rills have the effect of elongating the lawn and the foreground space. Beyond the lawn, the mass of strong verticals created by the silver trunks of the birches, both confuses our reading of the space and conceals the garden's boundary. The birches do not create a solid barrier but, instead, provide seductive glimpses of a landscape beyond. From another vantage point, fir trees form a dark backdrop to the lighter birches. The firs are situated in an adjoining field but they visually connect with the birches and so appear to be part of the garden. This cleverly designed landscape has the feel of a country park rather than that of a moderate-sized garden.

Fooling the eye does not necessarily require the use of an optical illusion. A different kind of deception was exploited by Isabelle C. Greene in her design for a garden in Santa Ynez, California. The property is a small, old, ranch-style house set among mature oaks in a gentle grassy valley. Greene's brief was to create a multi-recreational garden for a family who intended to use the house as a weekend retreat. Features to be accommodated included a swimming pool, large spa, tennis court, terrace, and car park. The challenge was to integrate these elements into the landscape in such a way that they would not detract from the natural and beautiful wild setting. Greene is renowned for her use

This natural-looking pond is not all that it seems. It is, in fact, a cleverly disguised swimming pool, created by the American landscape architect Isabelle C. Greene. Complete with a fake sandy beach, it is designed to integrate with the garden's natural landscape.

A freestanding yellow screen and architectural, large-leaved plants help to disguise the boundaries of this small garden in Miami. Designed by Raymond Jungles and Debra Lynn Yates, the cluttered scene implies the existence of hidden spaces.

of natural forms and understated, seemingly effortless design, and her solution was to conceal the features within the continuity of the existing landscape, allowing garden and wilderness to merge.

The most ingenious deception was reserved for the swimming pool – usually the most difficult garden feature to camouflage. Rejecting a hard rectangular form, Greene shaped the pool to nestle organically into the garden's natural valley. On one side, she has given it a gently sloping, imitation lakeside beach, on another, boulders emerge from the water to form a rocky embankment, which continues up a grassy slope. The "beach", which provides a paddling area for the younger children, is made from concrete, cast *in situ* and surfaced with fine sand held in a polymer dressing. Larger pebbles and stones casually litter the area to enhance the illusion of a natural shore.

Small garden spaces are a challenge, especially when the aim is to make them appear larger. One way to achieve this is to conceal or disguise the garden's boundaries – something that American landscape architect Raymond Jungles and his artist wife Debra Lynn Yates succeeded in doing in their own garden in Miami, Florida, in the late 1980s.

Jungles is an admirer of Brazilian landscape architect Burle Marx, whose gardens are hallmarked by the use of predominantly native plants

This very small garden in Brighton, England, was created by Roja Dove and Peter Causer, and is packed to overflowing with exotic plants and sculpture. Yellow and blue are the main colours used on artifacts and furnishings in the garden, and they act as foils to the planting of mainly evergreen foliage plants.

Opposite: **Declan Buckley's garden is narrow, with tall walls on all sides. To counter the sense of confinement and to make the garden appear wider, he has introduced strong horizontal lines in his layout of paving and pond.**

A path made of small slate "pebbles" leads the visitor along a tantalizing route through a jungle of planting that conceals the garden's boundaries. This is part of a garden designed by Declan Buckley, which, despite its exotic feel, is located in North London.

in an informal style, which allows his landscapes to merge with their South American surroundings. Yates and Jungles have collaborated on several garden projects. The Miami house is a single-storey dwelling, sitting centrally in the small urban plot, with the little remaining space containing an outdoor swimming pool.

The first task was to resurface the pool. A silvery blue-grey finish was used to make the water even more mirror-like and thus reflect the sky into the garden. The pool surround was made smaller and cut into an organic shape, making room for Jungles to create meandering paths that connected with a series of informal patios. The hard-landscaping and paths are loosely-laid paving slabs, with spaces for planting between.

The result is several gardens within the larger whole, with many obscured from immediate view. The garden is heavily planted, and large-growing, large-leaved, architectural plants dominate. Some original trees were retained and, combined with the new planting, conceal boundaries and link the garden with trees and vegetation outside the plot. The planting relies on foliage rather than flowers and, in true Burle Marx style, Jungles has selected native species, including palms, cycads, and bougainvillea.

Jungles and Yates's treatment creates the impression that the garden is much larger than its modest plot, and the large-growing plants contribute to this effect in three ways. Firstly, they are not what would be expected in a small garden, where the need to maximize space often means a more timid choice of plants. Secondly, they hide the wall and fence, and, thirdly, they act as living screens, breaking up the plot into a series of secret garden spaces. Colour is provided by Yates's abstract murals on sections of the perimeter fence, and by her ceramic mosaics on the masonry walls. Rather than emphasizing the boundary, as one might expect, the bold, colourful abstracts leap out visually and appear to be part of the garden landscape.

A jungle-style garden has been created in a very small space at a property in Brighton, England, a long way from the natural home of the

tropical plants that occupy it. The owners, Roja Dove and Peter Causer, have rejected the traditional English garden mix of shrubs and perennials in favour of exotic foliage plants. Some might argue that these will grow too large for such a small space, and, indeed, the effect of the large scale, dense planting – although bold and dramatic – is almost claustrophobic. Yet it is the planting that makes the plot seem larger than its true size.

Only 20m (65ft) square, the garden was originally a series of stepped concrete terraces which Dove and Causer removed, replacing the soil. Inspired by the Côte d'Azur in southern France, and preferring foliage to flowers, they aimed to make their garden lush and uninhibited. A small area of blue decking provides a place to sit within the jungle, while urns, plinths, and statuary of varied origins and eras peep out of the undergrowth. In more formal or conventional gardens, such *objets d'art* would be focal points, but here they are used to add a sense of mystery.

The planting provides effects at different levels. There are tall plants with distinct leaf shapes, such as cordylines and palms, which create an upper canopy. Below this are vertical bamboos and more rounded plants, such as *Fatsia japonica* and small-growing rhododendrons. The floor is smothered in shade-tolerant ground-cover, including ivies, epimediums, and *Polypodium vulgare* – a dwarf evergreen fern. There is an additional bonus in using tightly packed plants of this type: they are good sound absorbers, capable of reducing the noises associated with urban living. By shutting off and concealing their surroundings, Dove and Causer have created their own secret, intimate world, which would be easy to get lost in, despite its tiny size.

Unusual and distinctive plants have been used to great effect in North London. Unlike the Brighton plot, this garden is owned and was created by a professional garden designer, Declan Buckley. The garden

Above: A long gravel path leads invitingly through a seemingly overgrown garden in suburban Surrey. Trees, pergolas, and plants fill the moderate-sized garden to bursting point and conceal the gardens' boundaries in the process – the intention of its owners, Stephanie Grimshaw and Steve Leon.

Right: An ornamental mirror that once belonged to a piece of furniture hangs on the fence of the Surrey garden. The surprise feature adds another dimension to the space by suggesting that there is another garden through its frame.

was planned on paper before work commenced and, although only 22 by 6m (72 by 20ft), is now a lush imitation of a south-east Asian rainforest – a reflection of Buckley's long-standing interest in exotic plants. Visits to California, Sri Lanka, and North Vietnam established his plant preferences and subsequent planting palette. On his travels, he studied plants in their natural habitat – discovering what plants grew well with others – as well as the styles of gardens associated with Asia. For his own back garden, Buckley's aim was to conceal the boundaries to give the impression that the plot is larger than it is, and to create a garden full of mystery and surprise, with areas invisible from the house.

Immediately outside the house is a patio area, which is broader than it is deep and makes the space look wider than it actually is. A narrow

Large foliage plants placed in the foreground can conceal boundary fences or walls and prevent the whole of the garden from being seen from the house. This visual trick is demonstrated very effectively in this London garden designed by Jason Payne.

pond also spans the width of the garden and is crossed by a simple plank bridge. Only here are the boundary walls visible. Over the bridge is the start of a meandering path made of grey slate fragments. The path disappears into a dense mass of planting and leads to a hidden sitting area, shaded by a Sri Lankan monk's umbrella – a souvenir of Buckley's travels.

The garden, like Dove and Causer's in Brighton, is deliberately over-planted for instant effect, and Buckley used specimen-sized plants whenever possible to provide immediate height and screening. Large-growing plants with substantial foliage canopies were introduced to create shade and privacy. Many of the plants he has chosen also have a something of a reputation for rampant, invasive growth, including the many species of bamboos. Other planting includes astelias, arisaemas, and fatsias, with ground-cover provided by shade-tolerant ferns, alliums, and hellebores. A ceanothus with its seasonal abundance of rich blue flowers brings a different colour to the otherwise green space. Tree ferns placed near the windows create a foreground of foliage through which to view the garden from inside the house.

Trees can be surprisingly effective in a small garden, especially when those chosen might be regarded as too large for the space. Care must be taken in how close to a house they can planted, but this expertise and an obsession with trees is what Steve Leon and Stephanie Grimshaw have brought to their modest-sized garden in Chertsey, Surrey.

The garden, which measures 5 x 30m (16½ x 100ft), has evolved rather than been consciously designed, and so a natural informality has been retained. A circular pond divides the main patio from the planted garden, which is reached by a Japanese-style bridge. From the bridge, a path disappears into a dense plant-filled area, providing privacy and creating the impression that both path and plot stretch on forever.

The inclusion of a considerable number of trees is the most striking feature of the garden: Leon and Grimshaw's choice includes hazel, ash, *Gleditsia triacanthos* 'Sunburst', and three different types of eucalyptus – normally considered too large for a small suburban site. Their canopies merge with those in other gardens to give a sense of continuity.

At the end of the garden, the trees overhang a secluded sitting area, which has an unexpected feature. Set into part of the nearby fence are small windows, which frame views of the next-door garden, and allow Leon and Grimshaw to converse with their neighbours, with whom they are friends. Along the same fence, and close by, are framed mirrors, which reflect the garden. This combination of mirrors and clear glass is effective, being both deceptive and confusing.

At first glance, it appears that the garden continues through the architectural frame that spans this site in Islington, London. But the tree fern and house wall visible in the distance are reflected images, created by three large mirrors. The illusion is part of Marie Clarke's attempt to make a small garden appear larger.

Décollage
samedi 29 septembre !

Left: The sky is reflected in the glass panels that form the centrepiece of this extraordinary scene. Created by Patrick Blanc, the garden that surrounds the "sky mirror" has been planted up the wall of the building, and is kept alive by an ingenious watering system.

Right: The vertical garden is situated above the entrance to the Forum Culturel du Blanc Mesnil in Paris. The success of Blanc's garden proves that with the benefits of modern technology there is no limit to where a garden can be created.

Theatrical magic is often said to be "done with mirrors", and mirrors can be used in the same way in a garden. In the right context a large mirror can fool the eye into believing a garden extends beyond its true boundary. A substantial feature of this type is included in a small patio garden, designed by Marie Clarke in Islington, London. Three large, door-height mirrors are fixed to an architectural structure of rectilinear pillars and lintels, forming a series of elaborate door frames. The mirrors give the impression that the openings are entrances to a space beyond, but the "virtual" garden is simply a reflection of the real one. Planting near to and in front of the mirrors enhances the illusion by preventing the viewer from getting too close and by concealing the lower portion of the mirrors, which would inevitably become soiled and so spoil the effect.

In Paris, a French gardening magician practises deception of a different kind and on more than one victim – he tricks people and plants, and his gardens know no horticultural restrictions. Professor Patrick Blanc creates gardens on vertical walls. He does not use climbers, but instead employs shrubs and perennials that grow on the ground in ordinary gardens, including antirrhinums, sedums, irises, and geraniums, as well as ferns, bromeliads, and other epiphytes for shady sites.

His first vertical garden was created at his own house in a suburb of Paris, but his unique methods became public when he exhibited at the International Garden Festival at Chaumont. The inventor of the *mur vegetal* began his experiments as a child when he enriched water with nitrogen and encouraged orchids, ferns, and bromeliads to grow up his bedroom wall on capillary matting. As a student botanist, Blanc investigated how rainforest plants have adapted to grow on vertical surfaces, such as trees

and rock faces. He used this knowledge to create a nutritional irrigation system that can sustain garden plants on a similar plane.

Blanc creates his vertical gardens by constructing galvanized steel frames from which he hangs the planting medium – huge sheets of horticultural felt. The plants are inserted into simple strap-like pockets formed within the felt. The absorbent fabric takes in water and the essential growth nutrients from a refillable trough at the base. Water is also pumped to the top of the wall and allowed to trickle down. Nourished by this system, the roots of the plants intertwine to form a living mesh.

To deceive is not always the aim of a garden designer, and there are many gardens where a sense of a boundless space has been achieved, not by intent, but as a bonus and consequence of a designer's working method. Such is the case with the garden designed by New Zealander James Fraser for his partner, artist Biddy Bunzl. Fraser, whose distinctive

style is often described as "deliberate ramshackle", has created a garden that seems to be trying to escape from the confines of its Victorian London semi-detatched house site.

The garden area consists of a small section to the front of the house, and a rectangular space, the width of the house but twice as deep, to the rear. At the front, a dog-legged, loosely formed gravel path creeps through a mass of evergreen grasses, cherry tree trunks, bamboos, and spiky-leaved astelias. The path is outlined by weathered wooden posts, placed at random intervals along its length. There is a deliberate lack of definition, and the front fence, made of widely spaced, erratically arranged timbers, blurs the garden's edge, making it seem to spread and spill out.

At the back, a sea of plants replaces the customary lawn. Fraser's planting has an unregimented, left-to-nature appearance. Planting emerges through gravel, and the use of less structured plants, such as

Ramshackle fences, which are simply odd pieces of rotting timber sticking out of almost anarchic planting, make this garden in London seem as if it has never been touched. In fact, it was created by professional garden designer James Fraser, who deliberately tries to make gardens that look overgrown and unstructured.

grasses, adds to the informality. But naturalistic it isn't, since many of the plants, including tree ferns and *Astelia chathamica*, are exotics.

The hard-landscaping is sculptural and brutalistic. Walk-on surfaces are gravel or distinctive, ramshackle decking made from reclaimed wood. This heavily textured timber is also used for free-standing sculptural direction signs and for fences. An ornamental pool and a deck that butts up to the French windows are also made of timber. Beyond this, a meandering gravel path passes through the dense vegetation; for some of its length it rises off the ground as a narrow wooden walkway, as if crossing a bog, to pass over clumps of molina and other grasses.

It is the rambling, almost anarchic design that gives the garden its boundary-less appearance. Little respect has been paid to the confines of the space or its rectangular shape, and the house's architecture has not influenced the design in any formal way. Fraser has created a garden with strong impact, one that needs to be experienced and explored.

Deception in relation to a garden's boundary is frequently an issue of the site's small size. The creators of traditional Japanese gardens were also concerned with size, but in a different way. Many of the early Buddhist gardens were imitations, on a smaller scale, of real landscapes. Pruning and training trees was an essential part of Japanese gardening,

Above: This traditional Japanese "tour" garden is designed to deceive. The garden is experienced as a series of restricted and selected views arranged along a path. The lengthy journey along the prescribed route serves to give the impression that the garden is bigger than it actually is.

Opposite: A traditional Japanese garden is often a replica of a nearby natural landscape, and the garden's creators usually had to capture the spirit of the larger landscape in a miniature form. This bonsai garden in North London, created by Peter Sievert, is an attempt to emulate this practice.

Left: The Curtice Taylor garden, in the grounds of Jack Lenor Larson's house, The Longhouse, on Long Island, NY, is designed in the tradition of the long vista. A canal leads to a lawn avenue, which stretches towards a V-shaped opening in a freestanding wall.

Right: The "Red Garden" is one of a number of installations commissioned by Larson for The Longhouse. The bright red posts and similarly vibrant azaleas draw the eye forcibly to a focal point set in the woodland landscape.

not only to highlight a tree's natural shape but also to keep it from outgrowing the scale imposed by the garden landscape. The art of bonsai takes this process to its ultimate conclusion.

A complete garden of bonsai plants in a Japanese style has been designed and created in North London by Peter Sievert. The plants are perfect miniatures, with all the shapes and textures of their larger cousins. They contradict our sense of scale and space, and this effect is enhanced by Sievert's attention to detail, including a cleverly weathered rockery, and stone- and gravel-edged pools and waterfalls. The result is a convincing and disconcerting imitation of a life-size garden.

Artists have long been masters of deception. The ability to paint a convincing representation of the world through an understanding of perspective and the modelling of light and shade is a skill to be admired. The great *trompe l'oeil* masterpieces of the seventeenth-century Dutch painters are among the most revered. Twentieth-century artists were also

A blue neon light provides an alternative to the traditional rill to lead the eye not only across this contemporary landscape, but also towards the night sky above. The garden was designed by Dani Karavan, who regards himself as an artist rather than a landscape architect.

interested in fooling the eye, often with the intention of suspending disbelief. The surrealists Salvador Dalí and René Magritte, for example, turned a world that belongs in dreams into convincing landscapes.

Imagined landscapes are what Jack Lenor Larson, the respected textile designer, has introduced into his garden at The Longhouse on Long Island, New York. Since starting work on the garden in 1986, Larson has packed it full of sculptural features that are part art, part landscape.

One of his most stunning and surreal creations is the "Red Garden", which consists of a parallel row of rough-cut cedar trunks painted in brilliant red and set at equal distants apart. Between the trunks are planted scarlet azaleas. The red posts serve to intensify the natural red of the plants, and together they form a red avenue that draws the eye to a sculptural form nestling in the vegetation. The red contrasts starkly with the green of the grass and the surrounding shrubs and trees. This contrast gives the garden an almost supernatural presence in the woodland that it slices through, and it changes our understanding of the space it occupies.

Dani Karavan is an Israeli artist who specializes in environmental art, both as permanent and temporary installations. He has frequently created work that is difficult to categorize as either "art" or "landscape design". This dichotomy is evident in his design for the Dorfplatz, a public space situated between an historical residential area and the Communication Centre of Credit Suisse in Zurich. Created in 1995, Karavan's Dorfplatz can be interpreted as a contemporary landscape. It comprises familiar landscape elements including grass, water, planting, a terrace and sundial, all arranged within a formal, but modernist triangular pattern. Come nightfall, however, and our perception of the new landscape is dramatically altered when the most powerful element of the design becomes visible.

The focus of the garden is the minimal sundial, which is technically simply a gnomon and essentially a two-storey concrete post. Recessed into one side of the post is a neon tube that emits a blue light. The gnomon is connected visually to the terrace and garden floor by a concrete channel, down the centre of which is a continuation of the blue neon. At night, the beam of light links horizontal to vertical, rising upwards to connect the plaza with the stars and evening sky. Is it art or is it landscape? It is perhaps best described as a space-age version of the conventional long vista: one that links a man-made environment, not to the landscape beyond, but to the heavens above.

Dissolving the Edge

At Richmond, Mass., the landscape architect Susan F. Child used a series of lawn terraces, with minimal walls and steps, to integrate the house with the existing elements of the garden landscape, which include a quarry pool and a woodland. The lawn begins at the house, becoming a meadow as it reaches the pool.

In the eighteenth century, English garden designers such as William Kent reject the formal style associated with seventeenth-century France in favour of a more naturalistic approach. Although many of the great formal gardens, such as that created at Hampton Court Palace for King William and Queen Mary, had an informal wooded area with paths, called a "wilderness", these were sited well away from the residential buildings, which were usually fronted by parterre gardens and terraces. The English Landscape Movement, of which Kent was a pioneer, changed all this. Its followers rid the garden of the formal tradition, which they replaced with a picturesque style. By virtue of inventions such as the ha-ha, which they adopted and adapted from its formal origins, they were able to make their gardens appear to extend, unchecked, into the surrounding environment. Most significantly, the naturalistic landscape also came right up to the house. Heveningham Hall in Suffolk, is an example of this new style. Designed by "Capability" Brown, the landscape was brought up to the

For a house in Greenwich, Conn., artist and landscape designer Janis Hall used an expanse of rocks and stones to form the transition between the clean cut and prepared stone of the terrace and the organic landscape of the park-style garden.

house, without any formal boundaries, in the form of "an extensive park, which abounds in fine plantations and is diversified by a noble piece of water" (*The Beauties of England*, 1813).

Many contemporary designers have adopted this eighteenth-century philosophy, creating gardens where there is a subtle or even imperceptible transition from the house to the surrounding wild or rural landscape. Others believe that – for practical or aesthetic reasons – a more structured approach is required close to the house, but beyond this they seek a gradual transformation from the formal to the natural.

American landscape architect Susan F. Child has created many award-winning private gardens, and her design for a 20-ha (50-acre) property in Richmond, Massachusetts is one of her best. Child's aim was to make a garden that would not only be in harmony with its Berkshire environment but also a sympathetic response to the existing site, which comprised a Shaker-style farmhouse, a woodland, and a disused, water-filled quarry. Completed in 1987, the garden flows freely outwards from the house in a series of broad levels. A simple lawn terrace, which

The landscape of wind-blown dune grasses and occasional shrubs stretches up to the foot of this 1960s-style residence in Cape Cod. The scene looks natural but it is totally man-made, designed by A.E. Bye on land reclaimed from the sea.

includes a small patio bordered with herbs, begins at the house and continues, via a lawn ramp, to connect with a lower, sloping terrace (also lawn). From here, the ground descends as a meadow to the quarry pool.

The layout was created by sculpting the land between the house, pool, and woodland. The newly created lawn terraces and meadows are defined and retained laterally by dry-stone walls that descend with the sloping areas of lawn. Unobtrusive stone steps are introduced between the upper and lower lawns. Child's restraint is sympathetic with Shaker ideals, which value economy rather than ostentation. The planting is also minimal, with only an orchard and a few native nut trees to interrupt the horizontal lines and the visual movement from house to landscape.

Designer and sculptor Janis Hall opted to create a site-specific artwork rather than reshape the landscape when invited to design the garden of an American Georgian house in Greenwich, Connecticut. In response to the client's desire for low maintenance, Hall rejected a planting solution in favour of a landscape solution. Called "Murmuring Flow", it features a 100m (320ft) stream of stone that connects the house and its terrace to the garden's natural features. The sculpture of local boulders and rocks also relates the garden to the landscape beyond the site, which is characterized by rocky streams and woodland.

American Landscape architect A.E. Bye has no preference for any particular landscape but finds inspiration from the environment in which

Opposite: This dense woodland is the garden for a house in Connecticut, which was designed by A.E. Bye in the late 1970s. Nearer the house, the existing native trees and rhododendrons were thinned out but allowed to continue up to the windows.

Trees camouflage this cottage in Hertfordshire, and around it and lapping up to its walls is a garden, designed by Will Woodhouse, that combines naturalistic planting with a haphazard arrangement of stones. Although it functions as a domestic garden, its overgrown, stone-strewn landscape conceals its man-made origins and connects it to its surroundings.

he is working. His design solutions are often deceptively simple, giving the impression that nothing has been altered or that he has adopted what was already there. This is even true of his work at the Shapiro residence in Massachusetts, which was built on land that was originally below water. The site is a peninsula 122m (400ft) wide that projects 244m (800ft) into the sea at Cape Cod. It was established mostly with sand imported from an adjoining bay, and used to form mounds and valleys.

Bye was inspired by the features of the location, in particular the sand dunes. Because the site was established on sand, he knew it was essential that the planting was similar to typical coastal vegetation, and so he chose naturally hardy seaside plants; as a result the garden looks as if it is a continuation of the wider landscape. Bye strengthened this effect by limiting his choice of plants, using only five different types throughout the whole 3.25-ha (9-acre) site. Apart from the grasses that smother the undulating, sand dune-like forms, there are bayberry, pine, juniper, and yew. The dune grasses stabilize the ground's surface and unify its appearance. These grasses have grown from seed, and over the years the pine and bayberry have also self-seeded to make the garden appear even more natural. The garden has no obvious structure or focal points, and outdoor recreational space is restricted to the building's first-floor balconies and decks. The Shapiro residence emerges from the landscape, rather than being surrounded by it.

In sharp contrast to this seaside landscape at Cape Cod, the Leitzsch residence, near Ridgefield, Connecticut is a woodland site. Bye was asked to design the garden but his first instruction was that the balconies and decks of the house should be extended so that they projected

Indigenous rocks and stones are used by Molly Love to reinforce a sense of place in this garden in the Californian hills. The elevated location enables the garden to borrow a distant view, but here it is the delicate drifts of planting in the dry rock garden that allow the area as a whole to merge seamlessly with its more immediate surroundings.

Below: It is difficult to believe that this wildflower meadow is on the sloping roof of a house. This "garden" in France belongs to Jean Kling, who has used earth and planting as a natural form of roof insulation; this is a technique historically used in traditional Scandinavian houses.

Right: A low stone wall serves to link the stone-clad house to its garden landscape. A carpet of moss butts up to the house walls, forming part of the informal woodland landscape created by Keith Wagner for this hilltop property in Vermont, New England.

into the immediate surroundings. Views from the house to the distant landscape were then restored by the removal of a number of trees.

Bye's design has allowed the garden landscape to come right up to the house, so much so that trees touch the windows. The woodland garden is an extension of the natural environment, and additional trees are all native species, as are the shrubs that were added to bring seasonal colour. Bye believes that alien plants can have an adverse effect on the existing ecology of an area. By working with the woodland rather than imposing a preconceived design upon it, Bye created a landscape that merges imperceptibly with nature's own garden.

In some instances, a combination of design ideas achieves the desired effect. This is particularly evident in a garden created by designer Will Woodhouse for a cottage in rural Hertfordshire. Woodhouse combined an unusual use of local stone with a sympathetic planting strategy, so that the garden relates to and integrates with its rural environment.

The hedge that forms a boundary is carefully managed. Some individual trees within it, such as field maples, are allowed to grow tall,

Opposite: At the Meyer garden, designed by Oehme and van Sweden, and completed in 1989, a wooden boardwalk provides the only route through a sea of beach grasses and perennials. The dense planting begins at the house and stretches down to the shores of Lake Michigan.

Massed, close-knit groups of plants – here, rudbeckia, perovskia, and miscanthus cultivars – are the trademark of the American designers Wolfgang Oehme and James van Sweden.

and these give variety of height to the hedge line and frame views outside the garden. Small indigenous trees around the house have been retained and connect visually with the hedgerow, fields, and woodland beyond, thus allowing the garden to "borrow" a view.

The most eye-catching aspect of the garden is the abundant use of large, local chalk rocks and stones. In places the groups of standing stones, some upright some leaning, resemble the remains of a neglected, ancient stone circle. Elsewhere, the stones fulfil a more prosaic function: they define an ornamental pool and form a shallow waterfall. Collectively, the stones suggest a garden created out of a natural or "as found" landscape, rather than one imposed upon it.

A scheme that would marry their new property to its location was the requirement of the owners of a hilltop residence in Vermont. The house sits in 40ha (100 acres) of typical New England landscape, with woodland, wonderful views, and rich vegetation. The commission to design the garden was awarded to H. Keith Wagner, who completed it in 1996.

Like Bye, Wagner restricts his plants to a palette of indigenous varieties. The house was faced with local stone, and Wagner employed the same material in the garden for paths and walls. Instead of making a boundary, the walls were used to extend the architecture of the house into the landscape. To the front of the property Wagner installed a low, dry-stone wall to mirror the curved façade of the house. Set a short distance from the building, this is broken through in several places by new planting. A moss garden comes up to the house, as do a group of 17 white birch trees. Closely planted, the birches connect with maples and oaks to link the architectural order of the house to its organic surroundings. They are under-planted with ferns to suggest a continuation of the woodland floor. To the rear of the house, a large deck projects over the terrain to provide a recreational area from which steps lead down to untouched hilltop terrain.

At night the house is linked to its environment in a very special way. In the ground, Wagner has installed a narrow, galvanized trough, 15.25m

(50ft) long, which projects outwards from the building, below a glazed slit in the façade, and through the low garden wall. The trough contains small lights that are diffused through a frosted plastic cover, and in the evening, this slender band of light seems to extend the interior space of the house into the exterior world of the garden and its surroundings.

Acknowledged as the principal inventors of the "New American" garden, the landscape design partners Wolfgang Oehme and James van Sweden are renowned for their seamless planting schemes. Their work is recognizable by its loose, informal structure and the abundant use of colourful perennials and ornamental grasses, planted in merging masses. Wherever possible, native species are used, and emphasis is placed on seasonality in an attempt to create natural-looking schemes that are in tune with their surroundings. But Oehme and van Sweden's gardens do not imitate nature – rather, they capture the spirit of the natural landscape.

Oehme and van Sweden's design principle is based on a respect for the existing site and a reluctance to re-shape it. They also avoid the use of lawns, which van Sweden once described as "green concrete". The Meyer garden at Harbert, Mich., which was completed in 1989, when their innovative approach was first recognized, is representative of their style.

The site is a rolling hillside, which slopes down to nearby Lake Michigan. The garden is devoted almost entirely to expanses of the designers' trademark perennials and ornamental grasses. The choice of perennials includes types of hardy geraniums, as well as sedums, persicaria, salvias, and rudbeckias. Miscanthus and molina are the principal grasses, supplemented by wild dune grasses in a meadow that leads down towards the lake. Trees and shrubs, including pines, bamboos, dogwoods, cotoneasters, and amelanchiers, add organic structure, and sculptures are placed around the garden to provide the occasional focal point.

As one might expect, there is no lawn. Access through the sea of planting is provided by bark paths and wooden walkways that "fly" over the plants, without interfering with them. Both types of path create the impression that a wilderness has simply been made accessible. The planting comes right up to the house – the raised terrace on the lakeside elevation provides a place to admire a garden that seems to overwhelm the house and overrun the owner's tennis court, which is concealed behind large groups of *Miscanthus* x *giganteus*, pines, and dogwoods.

The home of Norm and Harriet Rotter, at Birmingham, Michigan, also has a garden that sweeps up to the house, but here its creator Randall K. Metz has employed a more structured, delineated style of planting. The new house is a modernist, single-storey building. Painted white, and angular in form, it was designed to contrast with the existing densely

Opposite: **In this garden, designed by Randall K. Metz, distinct curving bands of plants, distinguished by the variations in their foliage, begin at the foot of the walls of the house; they then follow the curve of the pathway, and merge with the surrounding woodland edge on the opposite side.**

Below: **Beyond the patio of this country house in Washington DC, the broad sweeps of perennial planting, designed by Oehme and van Sweden, create an impressionist-style landscape that dissolves into the distant countryside.**

wooded setting. The clients wanted to contribute to the site's inherent beauty and retain as many of the trees as possible, while Metz's aim was to unite the house to its surroundings.

His solution for the driveway and entrance path was to make free-flowing forms, foils to the angles of the house. The drive flows like a black river around the trees, while parallel white lines painted at intervals across it, link it to the geometry of the architecture. The similarly meandering path is a series of shallow-stepped black marble and sand terraces.

Metz chose plants with white flowers or white-variegated foliage to match the house, and restricted his palette to low-growing periwinkle, astilbes, and hostas, with some grasses. The scheme mimics the curving form of the driveway. Large areas of uninterrupted planting make a flowing pattern of organic shapes, defined by variations in foliage colour and low stone walls. The garden begins at the house and runs like a free-form parterre into the untouched remainder of the woodland.

On a hill in Santa Fe, New Mexico, is a garden created by designer Julia Berman and homeowners Andrew Ungerleider and Gay Dillingham. The house sits on the top of a ridge and boasts magnificent views of the distant Jemez Mountains. With the fence out of sight, the property inevitably borrows the view, but the site is made to appear boundary-less in other ways. By exploiting the steep terrain, Berman has created a modern version of the Japanese "tour" garden (*see p.14*).

Pathways dominate the layout, allowing it to be appreciated as an unfolding sequence of interconnected, yet isolated, experiences. Each vignette is designed to deny the visitor the opportunity to comprehend the overall shape or size of the area. The visitor entrance to the intensively planted garden is through a rustic arbour at the foot of the site. The route

Left: Strange egg-like sculptures sitting on a bed of creeping thyme, are flanked by a stepping-stone path, in the hilltop meadow at the Ungerleider garden in Santa Fe, New Mexico. The elevated location of the garden enables the view of the distant landscape to be borrowed.

Right: In the same garden, a mass planting of mixed grasses with splashes of colour from perovskia and white echinacea is redolent of the style of Wolfgang Oehme and James van Sweden. The prairie-like garden runs right up to the house and blends into larger shrubs nearby.

In a garden designed by Anthony Paul in Lucerne, the ornamental pool is bordered by irises. The pool becomes a stream crossed by a small wooden hump-backed bridge at its far edge, and the combined effect is to give the impression that the garden continues into the landscape.

to the house is along a path made of fragments of local sandstone, flanked by overflowing planted borders. A stone statue of Ganesha, the Hindu elephant god, announces the point where the path divides. One direction leads first to a shady, grape arbour and then to the herb-and vegetable-garden. From here, a series of stepping-stones returns visitors to the main path, which continues to the house via the hilltop "meadow".

Formed from earth removed during the excavation of the swimming pool, the meadow is spectacularly planted. Creeping lemon thyme fills the gaps between stepping-stones that cut across the meadow, which is smothered in a mass of perennials. Royal purple *Penstemon strictus*, white shasta daisies, and steely-blue grasses feature strongly, and the fusion of colour and texture is reminiscent of an Impressionist painting.

British garden designer Anthony Paul's preference is for foliage plants and their repeated use in large drifts. He employs this unfussy style to great effect in a garden above Lake Lucerne in Switzerland. Here, the large-scale planting helps the garden to merge with the surrounding vegetation, making a subtle transition from the man-made landscape to the wilder, untouched one beyond.

The garden contains several informal pools connected by timber walkways, creating an area of water near the garden's edge. Bordered by a wooden deck and a mass of irises and ornamental grasses, the mirror-like surface of the pool echoes the shimmering waters of the lake below, giving the garden a sense of place, by relating it to the lake, mountain, and sky.

Garden designers are not the only ones to seek to integrate house and garden with the surrounding landscape. Many architects also choose to work closely with the landscape, regarding it as an integral part of the conceptual development of a building. Olson/Sundberg, based in Seattle, have a reputation for environmentally-friendly architecture. The practice's best-known domestic project is a house on a hillside above Filucy Bay, at

This "lawn", topped with projecting architectural forms is the roof of a house designed by architects Olson/Sundberg at Filucy Bay in Washington State. The lawn serves to integrate the contemporary-style house with both the immediate and the distant surroundings.

A natural cliff-top landscape of wildflowers and trees has been adopted for the roof of this unusual house, designed by architect Obie Bowman, at Sea Ranch, California. Completed in 1987, this design is a benchmark in the successful integration of architecture and the landscape.

at Longbranch, Washington State, designed for a former American Ambassador to Iceland. At Longbranch, Olsen took the idea of the garden "lapping up" to the house a step further: he allows the landscape to pass through and over the building as an inseparable element of its design.

Completed in the late 1960s, the basically rectilinear building is softened by its unusual relationship with the land. The single-storey, flat-roofed residence is built as two stepped levels, inserted into the sloping hillside so that the roof of the upper level supports a continuation of the surrounding vegetation. The roof of the lower level is a lawn – a solution that is reminiscent of the sod-roofed houses found in Iceland. The living area on the upper level is cave-like and sheltered, while on the lower space, which has floor-to-ceiling windows and a projecting, decked balcony, advantage is taken of panoramic views of the nearby Filucy Bay.

Architect Obie Bowman is also committed to a more environmentally-friendly architecture, for reasons both functional and aesthetic. His buildings are designed to be energy efficient and to be visually non-detrimental when built in a natural landscape. The Brunsell residence at Sea Ranch, California, is typical of Bowman's approach.

Completed in 1987, the broadly V-shaped house is in a meadow on a cliff top, emerging out of its natural setting. The walls reflect the local vernacular style and are clad in timber, but the roof is less conventional – it rises from the tips of the two wings of the "V" at ground level, forming a flat plane over which the excavated meadow has been reinstated and allowed to grow. Although only part of the house is subterranean, Bowman has used an earth berm to give the impression that most of it is underground. The meadow roof acts as a form of temperature control for the interior and provides the occupants with a rooftop wildflower garden. This is a perfect expression of the garden design concept of "dissolving the edge" since the house and its natural surroundings are, quite literally, as one.

The Garden Trouvé

A boardwalk zigzags its way into a wetland in this garden at Grande Island, Vermont. It is representative of designer Susan F. Child's strategy for the site, which involved only minor interventions into the existing natural landscape.

In the world of art, the term *objet trouvé* (found object) is used to describe an artifact that has been given artistic status simply by adoption or through a minimum of creative intervention. The French artist Marcel Duchamp invented this idea of "ready-made" when he exhibited a bottle rack as a sculpture in 1915. It was the beginning of conceptual art, a form that requires no production and exists solely as an intellectual proposition.

Interpreted more liberally, the concept of the "found object" has influenced the development of landscape design. It has encouraged a new generation of garden designers to adopt a more environmentally-aware approach. Instead of imposing new forms on the natural landscape, often to its detriment, they now design alongside nature with minimal intervention. This "design by adoption" is respectful to both the environment and the ecology of the site. The gardens are boundary-less since they are simply continue the existing landscape.

One of the best known and most impressive of these "ready-made" gardens is that created by American landscape architect Susan F. Child for a residence in Vermont. The site is an 32-ha (80-acre) stretch of land on a high peninsula on Grande Island, overlooking Lake Champlain. The property contains a variety of landforms and vegetation: there is a headland with a shale cliff and white cedar trees, a sloping beech woodland that drops down to a wetland of birch and maple, a grassy cove and beach, and, further afield, a high and expansive meadow. The ground throughout the site is covered with a diverse range of delicate vegetation, including blueberries and ferns.

The client's brief required Child to unify all the elements of the existing landscape into a cohesive garden, but to do so with as little visible change as possible to the natural features. Child's solution consists of a collection of viewing platforms, boardwalks, wooden steps, and pavilions, which link the building loosely with its natural surroundings. The boardwalks stretch unobtrusively from the house's timber viewing platform, and provide access through the property with minimum interference – one floats over the wetland like a pier. These raised paths prevent the vegetation from being damaged while encouraging visitors to explore the garden's

Above: A raised timber walkway ends with a small viewing platform that offers views across the waters of the Hood Canal on Olympic Peninsula, Washington State. Very little of the natural landscape was disturbed in the construction of the walkway and the house it joins on to (*see below*).

Right: This timber-constructed house was designed by the architect James Cutler, and is raised above the ground on stilts. The garden is formed simply from the unspoilt natural surroundings, left as found.

natural features. The platforms and pavilions are placed along the cliff top to highlight views, while the steps allow access to the lake's shore. A series of connected experiences, the garden is devoid of any grand plan. It is a subtle landscape, with no precise beginning or end.

James Cutler, an American architect, is committed to the protection of the environment – a stance that has influenced his design work. Cutler, who is based in Bainbridge Island, Washington, hopes that his nature-sensitive architecture will encourage his clients to appreciate the landscape and, wherever possible, he seeks to bring the occupants of his houses into close proximity with nature. His manifesto is given concrete form in a house he designed in the densely forested Olympic Peninsula in Washington State. Only three trees had to be removed for the construction of the building, which is perched on a 60-m (200-ft) high bluff overlooking the Hood Canal. The timber-constructed house rests on the ground at the top of the rise, where it is surrounded by indigenous rhododendrons.

A timber pier allows visitors to enter a boggy creek at Sweet Farm, in Quebec. It is part of a renovation of an existing landscape by PLANT, whose strategy was to highlight and make accessible areas of particular interest.

A bright red wooden walkway weaves its way down through the sparse vegetation of a rugged and inhospitable landscape in Chile. Nearby is a hotel designed by architect German del Sol, who wished guests to experience the "natural beauty" of the hotel's formidable surroundings.

Where the ground drops away to the north, towards the canal, it is supported on a series of stilts that eventually project it some 4.5m (15ft) above the ground. The driveway and garage block, situated 40m (130ft) from the house on the south side, are connected to the front door by a long, wooden bridge. This straight walkway continues through the house as a hallway, to emerge on the north-facing side as a raised timber pier, 14.5m (48ft) long. The structure passes through a dense group of alder trees before culminating in a viewing platform, from where steps lead down to the forest floor and the waters of the Hood Canal.

Thanks to its timber-stilt construction, Cutler's house makes only minimal contact with the ground. Substantial and damaging excavation of the existing landscape for footings and foundations was not required, while the elevated walkways and decks allow its owners to be in close contact with the surrounding environment, without interfering with it.

A similar solution is used on a farm in Canada. Sweet Farm is an estate of 34.5ha (85 acres) at Eastern Townships, in Quebec. The forested area contains meadows, cliffs, and gorges. In 1994, the owners commissioned the landscape architects PLANT – Lisa Rapoport, Christopher Pommer, and Mary Tremain – to intervene and make it more usable.

The design team's intention was to highlight the existing, varied, natural and man-made features and to enable the owners to experience the subtleties of the rich environment. They discovered that the site was a mixed topography, full of relics of domestic, industrial, and agricultural life. Following a detailed survey, Rapoport and Pommer identified places and features of special interest, and they decided to link these by various types of pathway, depending on the nature of the terrain. Some paths are simply deer runs turned into tracks, while others are made of wooden "stepping-stones". Wooden walkways allow access into more boggy areas, and a pier leads visitors into a creek. In one place, a cliff-top path ends in a wooden platform that projects over the cliff edge and into the tree canopies. The paths are not intended as tourist routes to places of interest, but are simply methods of encountering the ordinary and commonplace. Some of the relics from the estate's previous life are exploited and built upon: a

An apparently ad-hoc arrangement of timbers and steel bars thrusts this balcony and canopy through and over a tropical-looking landscape. This house in Brisbane is designed by the architect Rex Addison, who built it within an existing and overgrown garden.

stack of rusting mink cages has been used to create a moss-floored room, and a discarded car has been turned into a sculptural object. The sequential journey through the estate is designed so that the owners and any visitors can rediscover the natural, historical, and social wonders of an existing landscape, rather than find themselves presented with a new one.

Walkways feature prominently in the landscaping for a hotel at San Pedro de Atacama in Chile. The hotel's architect, German del Sol, has turned the surrounding rugged and inhospitable terrain into a nature trail. A red-stained wooden deck leads guests down a sparsely vegetated ravine and over a series of waterfalls, which are often dried up in the summer. As at Sweet Farm, the walkway allows visitors to appreciate an untouched natural landscape, but here it also keeps them at a safe distance from snakes and other creatures that frequent the area.

When Australian architect Rex Addison decided to design and build himself a new house, he located it within an established domestic garden – a sub-tropical garden at Taringa, in Brisbane, which surrounds the original family home, and was begun by Addison's grandfather in the 1920s. The garden overflows with lush planting; many of the palms and ferns have overgrown – and now conceal – walls and terraces built years earlier to make the most of the sloping site. Over a footbridge, which crosses a gully, and hidden among trees is the second building to be erected on the site: the architect's studio. The third building, Addison's new house, is similar to the studio and can best be described as a sort of de-constructivist treehouse. Raised on legs above the sloping site, it is an eccentric mix of decks, gables, bays, and corrugated metal canopies, but in essence, it is a timber framework clad with a plywood skin. Like the studio, it is also set among the trees and overgrown plants of the garden.

The seemingly intuitive, rather than pre-planned, design of the house allows it to zigzag through and sail over existing natural and man-made elements. The construction's red timber columns add an additional feature at ground level, while open-decked, projecting balconies above provide the architect and his family with access into the site's exotic canopy. Inside the house, there is a sense of nature trying to break in, with the plants seemingly responsible for its shambolic appearance.

Swiss architects Jacques Herzog and Pierre de Meuron are known for their sensitive response to the environment in which they are working, be it rural or urban. When they were commissioned to design a house at Tavole in the Ligurian Mountains of Italy, Herzog and de Meuron stuck to their principles and came up with a solution that allows the new structure to sit comfortably within its rural environment. The three-storey residence, built on an old stone terrace, projects from a rocky promontory and seems to emerge naturally from a hillside of abandoned olive groves, criss-crossed with dry-stone walls. The architects have related the essentially modernist house to these dry-stone walls by facing its exterior with panels made of richly textured local stone and without the use of mortar. Stone retaining walls also form a series of grass-and-stone terraces in the garden. According to the architects, the local stone carries with it

Almost concealed by the old olive groves on a hillside at Tavole, in Italy, this modern house, designed by Herzog and de Meuron, offers views of the surroundings in a style similar to that of a fifteenth-century Italian villa.

Steps and pathways lead around the garden of this house perched on the top of a rocky outcrop in the Stratton Mountain region of Vermont. The garden's designer, Chris Dunn, opted to make the most of the existing landscape rather than change its character.

"an imprint of the local weather and vegetation". It roots the house to its locality, physically, ecologically, and historically. This is a house that could be said to be on intimate terms with its landscape.

To construct a new house on the side of a hill in the Stratton Mountain region of Vermont, a large cut had to be made into the rocky terrain, leaving a visible scar when the building was completed. Wanting to repair the damage, the owners of the property, Bill and Carolyn Stutt, employed the services of landscape architect Chris Dunn. The client's brief demanded the restoration of the natural landscape, and a design that would wed the house to its dramatic natural location. Dunn realized that further intrusions into the terrain to create architectural landscape features, such as terraces, would conflict with the powerful form of the house and disrupt the area even further. The rocky ground also restricted what could be achieved. Dunn's design solution is eloquent, sensitive, and wonderfully simple. It is a mixture of two components identified as

The small structure nestling among trees is a sauna. Designed by architect David Salmela, this geometric building is at home in its natural setting, a lakeside woodland in Minnesota.

"mountain" and "forest". "Mountain" was conceived as being rugged and rocky, with no planting; "forest" was seen as a softer landscape, with trees, shrubs, ground-cover, and grasses, all of which would be in keeping with the natural surroundings.

Along the forest-facing side of the single-sweep drive that leads to the front of the property, Dunn planted white spruce, birch, viburnum, and ground-covering fescue grass to create a soft, natural-style landscape. In contrast, on the other side of the drive, the exposed rock ledges of the excavated ground are deliberately left unplanted. Around the house, low-growing blueberry and bunchberry are planted up to the walls to link the building to its site. Away from this area, part of the garden has been developed into an alpine meadow, with planting between the cut-rock ledges, and, from here, a stone stairway leads to a deer path that forms a route around the garden.

A desire not to spoil a natural woodland was the intention of architect David Salmela when asked to design a sauna on the estate of a private house in Minnesota. The modest geometric architecture, Finnish in inspiration, does not upstage the surroundings, and the structure nestles

comfortably in the clearing within the mixed woodland. The new landscaping is restricted to a paved pedestal, on which the structure sits, and a retaining wall. The rest of the clearing is restored as an area of grass that is allowed to dissolve into the surrounding woodland.

The Sumner House, at Puento Soivio in Vammala, Finland, has a relationship with its surroundings that is very different to that of the sauna in Minnesota. Designed by Siren Architects, the house is a bridge spanning a rock-strewn river. The bridge supports are the building's only contact with the ground and they allow the landscape to flow, quite literally, up to and under the house. The single-storey building occupies space above the natural vegetation, which remains untouched. Looking from the house, the course of the river provides open vistas in both directions.

As Sumner House proves, it is perfectly possible to create a property that respects the environment of which it is part. An even greater achievement can be found in a project that involved not one but many houses. This was the challenge accepted by landscape architect Lawrence Halprin, when he was asked to plan Sea Ranch, in Sonoma County, California. Set between cliff tops and upland forests, north of

Opposite: **A bridge is a house in Vammala, Finland. Sumner House, designed by Siren Architects. The single-storey timbe-and-corrugated metal structure spans a river and provides its residents with unsurpassed views of the river and woodland, as well as the wildlife that inhabits this landscape.**

Right: **Sumner House nestles within a natural landscape of birch trees and sedges. The architectual team's aim was to design a building that would not distract from, or disturb, its beautiful surroundings. The garden is simply nature as found.**

San Francisco, Sea Ranch is a residential area of some 2,000 homes on a site of 2,023ha (5,000 acres). Yet this development is very different from typical American out-of-town housing, with not a manicured lawn in sight.

Designed to strict codes, the houses are in the spirit of the local vernacular style, with features including redwood cladding and steeply pitched roofs to make them resemble agricultural buildings. Halprin's work was completed in the early 1960s and is now seen as being ahead its time in its ecological awareness. His plan was based on a sense of location and was intended to place the houses in partnership with the landscape.

In his early years, Halprin worked with Thomas Church, a pioneer of the "Californian style", a response to both the demands of modern life and the challenge of steep hillsides and irregular-shaped plots. During this time, Halprin developed a desire to preserve natural settings. He was one of the few of the "new" generation of modernist landscape architects who sought to design in harmony with the land, rather than in conflict with it. Halprin's vision for Sea Ranch was, in his own words, an "experiment in ecological planning", somewhere "where wild nature and human habitation could interact." He was determined to avoid suburbia at all costs.

The houses are arranged in T-shaped clusters – rather than in straight lines facing the sea – and are like separate villages, each wrapped around

A meadow of wildflowers and native grasses stretches up to a plain timber-clad house, which is located within an innovative residential development designed in the 1960s by Lawrence Halprin, at Sea Ranch, California. Here, there are no obvious driveways and domestic front gardens; instead, the existing natural landscape is preserved.

three sides of a meadow. Half of the development is open to the public, with mowed trails cut into the grass to provide access to the shoreline of cliffs, beaches, and tidal pools. Roads and service facilities are low-key and virtually unnoticeable. The natural landscape, a mix of tall grass meadows, rocky outcrops, and wind-blown, sculptured trees, is retained as much as possible, and even conceals a golf course. Where windbreaks were needed, Halprin planted hedges of native cypress, and all other new planting is also of indigenous varieties.

Sadly, Halprin's design was implemented on only 600ha (1,483 acres) of the development. However, what exists here is a landscape for a community, rather than an individual – a preservation of a natural landscape that can be enjoyed by all.

Richard Haag is an American designer who also likes to work with the land in a subtle way. He prefers to make minor intrusions and alterations, which can still change a landscape dramatically. In 1978, Haag won a competition to create a series of four gardens at the Bloedel Reserve, an estate of 61ha (150 acres) near Seattle, Washington State. Bloedel was a timber magnate and began the garden project in 1951, inviting numerous designers to submit plans. His main desire was that the gardens should be places of contemplation, rather than botanical exercises.

Haag's four gardens alternate between formal landscapes and seemingly natural and untouched spaces. A sense of the land "as found" is particularly evident in his moss garden, which is situated within an ancient grove of alders and conifers. Haag had the existing ground-covering salmonberry plants removed and replaced them with 275,000 plugs of Irish moss. Some of the very old alders were removed or reduced until just their trunks remained. Fallen trees – some cut down in the 1880s, when they were already over 600 years old – were left on the floor to rot and host mosses. This is a "non" space, according to Haag, designed to activate all the senses, and it is also an organic space – one that appears to have evolved through natural processes rather than created by human intervention.

The moss garden at the Bloedel Reserve looks like a natural landscape; the woodland floor is littered with fallen trunks, covered by a carpet of moss and ferns, and illuminated by what little light penetrates through the canopies of the remaining trees. Although the trees are original, the moss and ferns are all imported by landscape architect Richard Haag.

Above right: **This group of inscribed stones is a work by the poet and sculptor Ian Hamilton Finlay. Called "The Present Order", the collection of 11 rough-cut stones form a quotation from the French revolutionary, Saint Just: "The present order is the disorder of the future." Looking at the statement then the landscape in which the stones rest can be very thought provoking.**

Left: **A dark slate form reminiscent of a submarine conning tower intrudes into this unspoilt Scottish scene of hill-top lake and grassland. Entitled "Nuclear Sail"and created by Ian Hamilton Finlay, it is an example of how emblematic sculpture can add new meaning to an existing landscape.**

Ian Hamilton Finlay is a poet, sculptor, and gardener, and has chosen the garden as his principal means of expression. His own garden, at Little Sparta, near Dunsyre in the Pentland Hills of Scotland, is his most comprehensive project. It is a re-working of the "emblematic" garden, which was particularly popular in Roman and Renaissance times. The philosophy behind this kind of garden is that the association of plants and inanimate objects may be considered on two levels: the garden could be enjoyed simply in terms of its shapes, colours, and composition; but it may also be interpreted on an intellectual level in that each element has symbolic value.

Finlay enjoys the power of the written word and its use dominates the sculptural and architectural forms that are placed about this landscape. The garden is a series of places, some formal and cultivated, others left untouched and natural. There are pools and woodland areas, as well a front garden and a Roman garden. What is consistent is the inclusion of artifacts and inscribed stones within these spaces.

There is much wit in Finlay's superbly crafted stones. An inscription on a free-standing stone placed next to a plantation of young sycamore trees reads, "Bring back the birch." Elsewhere, a stone tablet hangs from the branch of a tree like a giant botanical label, and carries the signature of the early sixteenth-century German artist Albrecht Dürer. Around the bases of birch trees in the temple garden, Finlay has placed cut-stone plinths, out of which the trees appear to grow like columns.

In an uncultivated area, near a small lake, the landscape is given new meaning with the introduction of sculpture entitled "Nuclear Sail" in the form of a submarine's conning tower; its distinctive form seems to threaten the peace of this beautiful and isolated part of Scotland, the untouched surroundings adding to the pertinence of the work.

Mimicry

This wildflower meadow drifts down into a mill pond in a scene that is regarded as typical of rural England. However, the meadow isn't natural – it is an imitation created by Julie Toll, an expert in wildflower gardening, at a farm house in Hertfordshire.

There are many ways to conceal the boundary of a garden and many methods to integrate the garden with its environment. The intention might be to exploit the surroundings as an essential element of a garden's design, or it might be to use them to make the garden look larger. One of the most satisfying and subtle approaches does not rely on architectural features; instead, the designer creates a garden that mimics its surroundings. Rural, agricultural, and even seascapes have been imitated in this way to great effect.

Natural wildflower meadows or woodlands are much admired, and, luckily, there are still areas where such landscapes exist. Although many have been lost to industrial-scale agricultural practice and suburban expansion, the recent decline in farming in Britain has slowed this loss, while the "set aside" policy takes land out of production and allows it to revert to the wild. Farmers are also being encouraged to become "guardians" of the countryside. As a result of the decline in farming, many farms are no longer worked, and barns have been converted into living quarters. The more this happens, the more inevitable it becomes that the adjoining landscapes also change from agricultural to domestic.

Too often the old farmsteads are "suburbanized" by their new owners, with manicured lawns and city-style planting leading to a loss of the building's sense of place and history. Fortunately, the new owners of a farm in Hertfordshire wanted to preserve its history and make a garden appropriate to the setting. They bought Jenningsbury Farm in 1992, and set about creating a garden in the 1.6-ha (4-acre) paddock that adjoins the house. They excavated a pool and dredged the ancient moat that enclosed the paddock on three sides – this is thought to have surrounded a much grander house that once stood on the site.

A wildflower meadow was high on the agenda, and the owners employed British designer Julie Toll, who is a master at creating such

Landscape architect Fernando Caruncho's estate at Mas de les Voltes in Spain has a formal garden with a difference. In this view a circular pool is at the starting point of a grassy avenue, flanked by olives and columnar cypresses that define large geometric "borders" of wheat.

gardens, and works almost exclusively with wildflowers. Toll spent her formative years on a farm in Worcestershire, and has grown up with an appreciation of how cultivated and natural landscapes can merge.

The meadow was only part of Toll's scheme for the farm. She deemed it important that areas nearer to the house should be treated differently, and designed a garden that is a gradual transition from "cultivated" to "wild". Near the farmhouse, the garden is structured, with clearly defined flower beds. Here, the grass is cut close and "garden"-type plants dominate. Further away from the house is an intermediate zone, with some parts designated as frequently mown, and others as expanses of longer grass, containing tough cultivated plants such as *Rosa rugosa* and crocosmia. Linked to this area is a woodland walk that leads to and along the moat. Finally, there is the meadow and pool.

At the farm, the soil is rich and soggy and thus not ideal for the classic wildflower planting, which prefers well-drained soil on chalk.

The area was also infested with perennial weeds. Toll's first tasks were to improve the soil and deal with the weeds. The wildflowers, which are species only, were introduced as seeds and as "plug" plants. The planting includes vetch, cranesbill, clover, bedstraw, and agrimony, dispersed among fine grasses, with woundwort, foxglove, rattle, and briony used to fill the more shady wooded edges of the meadow. Ox-eye daisies and long meadow grass lead down to the pond, where the marginal and boggy areas are planted with a mix of astilbes, primulas, geums, and loosestrife. Toll avoided introducing too many different species, which can result in a contrived and unnatural look, and she placed great emphasis on the use of grasses. Mown paths through the meadow allow the owners and visitors to enjoy the flowers close to hand.

A typical and romantic feature of the countryside appears to have been recreated, but this is not a genuine meadow, rather an imitation of one. Toll has worked with nature to create a feature that seems inseparable and indistinguishable from the farm's natural, rural environment. However, a wildflower garden requires a great deal

A lawn with an irregular edge forms the transition between an ornamental herbaceous border and regimented rows of lavender in this ranch garden in the Californian hills. Designed by Ron Lutsko, the crop-style layout of the lavender relates the garden to its agricultural surroundings.

of management – if left to nature it would soon become overgrown and colonized by unwanted stronger species.

While Toll is inspired by the natural environment, the Spanish landscape architect Fernando Caruncho prefers the agricultural landscape. His gardens belong to the Spanish-Moorish formal tradition and also owe a debt to André Le Nôtre, the seventeenth-century French garden designer, who was employed at Versailles. Caruncho's formal landscapes are very different from those of his early predecessors, however: he combines the aesthetics of the past with forms associated with the shaping of the landscape for agricultural purposes, drawing inspiration in particular from irrigation features and ancient farm patterns.

On his estate at Mas de les Voltes in Spain, completed in 1994, Caruncho created a formal garden that mimics its surroundings. He took agricultural features such as traditional crops, harvesting equipment, and water-collection tanks, and arranged them in a formal composition that mixes style with function. Crops such as wheat, fruit trees, and vines

At Mas de Pilons, France, this meadow garden, designed by Tim Rees, presents the visitor with a series of horizontals. A wide expanse of lawn becomes a crop of lavenders, which dissolves into a polychromatic field of wildflowers.

An avenue of plane trees ends in an architectural focal point in a manner reminiscent of a formal French garden. This example at Mas de Pilons provides welcome shade alongside the informal meadow garden.

are set within a geometric pattern that also includes formal beds, well-maintained lawns, and pools. Terraces of grapes surround a square of four identical pools separated by mowed-grass avenues. These avenues, which are lined by olive trees alternating with columnar cypresses, also define the triangular and rectangular fields of golden wheat and extend into the distance. The clearly defined agricultural elements reinforce the formality of the landscape yet, by their imitation of another man-made environment, they also connect the garden visually with the more conventional working farmland of its immediate surroundings.

At a ranch south of San Francisco Bay the challenge that faced landscape architect Ron Lutsko was to create a garden that would be in keeping with its surroundings – a landscape of rocky outcrops and rolling hills, adopted wherever possible as farmland. Lutsko's solution is similar to the Caruncho garden in that it also contains a visual reference to the agrarian landscape. Rather than create a stylized agricultural landscape, however, Lutsko prefers to hint at crop patterns and echo them in the manner in which he sets out garden plants.

The site covers about 0.2ha (½ acre) and was completed in 1990. The house is not always occupied, so it was essential that the garden would look after itself. The antithesis of Julie Toll's wildflower garden, this planting is resilient, self-sustaining, and demands little maintenance; it is strong enough to withstand drought conditions, intense heat, and frost, as well as invading deer and even stray cattle. The design comprises four interrelated areas that extend outwards from the house

Above: A square of water and numerous identical squares of meadow planting within an orchard provide an unusual formal interpretation of the meadow garden. This example was created by Sylvie and Patrick Quibel at Côte Jardin in the late 1990s.

Opposite: A wooden walkway zigzags along a ditch in this wildlife garden, located in Kilcot, Gloucestershire, and partly designed by Julie Toll. The "fish out of water" were designed and made by craftsman John Daniels.

towards the adjoining landscape, and each area is less formal than the one preceding it.

The first area, located alongside the house, is a composition of simple geometric patterns that relate to the architectural plan of the building. The planting is a mixture of hardy shrubs and perennials, which are domestic in scale and confined within clearly defined areas. The second area is a lawn, which is cleanly shaped near the house but irregular where it meets the staggered edge of a paved terrace. It is after the paving, in the third area, that the garden is linked to the agricultural landscape immediately beyond. Here, Lutsko has used drought-tolerant ornamental lavenders in well-defined rows to mimic the nearby fields. A distinctly utilitarian stockfence connects rather than separates the "crop" of lavender from the agricultural crops beyond. A fourth area, consisting of grasses and native vegetation, is planted in a manner that reflects the landforms and plant masses of the distant uncultivated landscape, completing the integration of the ranch garden with its environment.

A garden at Mas De Pilons in the Provence region of France, also has agricultural references. There are olive trees, a spring meadow, and rows of lavender, all of which can be admired from under the shady canopy of an avenue of plane trees. This is one of many meadow-style

The vast flat horizontal character of the landscape of the Argentine pampas has been worked with rather than against in this design for the garden of the estate of El Choique Viego. In essence it is a broad lawn, interrupted by eucalyptus trees and groups of low-growing plants.

gardens created in France, where it might be assumed that garden design would be dominated by the country's formal tradition. In fact, France has a long history of naturalistic gardens, dating from medieval times.

The factor that has generated a renewed interest in this informal style of garden is *friche* (fallow agricultural land). Contemporary meadows are not cottage gardens but large areas of abandoned pasture and fields that have been transformed into gardens. Their creators have used a number of methods, including simply mowing existing grass and adding bulbs and perennials, or sowing seed mixes. These gardens are managed and maintained, but many retain a sense of the original land use because they are not overly designed. They are agricultural-style meadows rather than wildflower gardens.

Provence has history of meadow agriculture, despite its dry Mediterranean climate and poor soils. For centuries it has been a patchwork of tiny fields, with areas of grazing land on less fertile, stony hills. Today, abandoned olive-tree terraces characterize the coastal Mediterranean area, while in upland northern Provence little remains of the sheep pastures that once produced natural lavender and other aromatics. In the irrigated and richly fertile valley land around Saint-Rémy-de-Provence near Tarascon, productive meadows still flourish as market gardens, and there is an abundance of fields of single crop, seed-grown annuals, such as poppies and sunflowers.

The meadow garden at Mas de Pilons is in this region and was created by English designer Tim Rees. He has planted 5,000 sq. m. (53,820 sq. ft) of wildflower meadow by sowing a mix of grasses and perennials, supplemented with annuals as a nursery crop and to suppress weed growth. Combined with regular rows of lavender and the olive plantation, this is an agricultural, rather than garden, landscape, and one that is part of a much broader historic scene.

A variation on this concept of the meadow garden can be found at a nursery near Rouen, in northern France. Here, the geometry and order associated with orchards or market gardens has inspired a more formal approach. Created by Sylvie and Patrick Quibel, the Côte Jardin was begun in 1997, and the finished result is as much land art as garden. The simple design consists of a long central stretch of frequently mown grass which also contains a square reflecting pool, and a formal apple orchard, set among equally spaced, identically sized squares of meadow. The squares are clearly defined by the mown grass that separates them, and their regimented arrangement contrasts with the haphazard planting of grasses and flowers that grow within each of them.

The planting at the El Choique Viego estate, designed principally by John Brookes, is mainly grouped around rocky outcrops and a lake. It is a mix of hardy herbaceous plants, including rudbeckias and pennisetums.

An unusual house demands an unorthodox landscape. George Hargreaves has provided just that for this post-modernist-style residence in the Napa Valley. With its series of rings and serpentine bands of contrasting grasses, the design is as much land art as it is landscape design.

A different continent, country, and climate, and a very different landscape have inspired the design of a large garden for J&M Mulville in Argentina. The estate of El Choique Viego is situated at Sierra del Tandil, south of Buenos Aires. The 0.8-ha (2-acre) site on the Argentine pampas is a typical prairie – a flat landscape with rocky outcrops. The vast open expanses and strong horizontals of this arid environment have been taken on board by the garden's designers, the Argentine Juan Grimm, and John Brookes from Britain, who was principally responsible for the planting.

From the house, which sits on a low knoll, an expanse of mown lawn sweeps down to merge with the wild grassland beyond. Eucalyptus trees planted by the early settlers provide windbreaks and break up the flat plane. The upper lawn is dotted with acacia trees to provide shade near the house, act as foreground planting, and create a transition between the house and uncultivated landscape.

In keeping with the emptiness and openness of the garden's environment, the planting is deliberately sparse, restricted mainly to areas adjacent to the rocky outcrops that are a feature of the estate. Pampas grass, so often seen in single clumps as an ornamental plant in suburban front gardens, is planted *en masse* here, and, mixed with smaller-growing grasses and wildflowers, creates the impression of a natural prairie landscape.

A post-modernist-style house situated on an exposed hill in the Napa Valley region of the United States demanded a garden that reflected the spirit of the building's unorthodox architecture. The house was designed by London-based architects Powell-Tuck, Conner, and Orefelt. The landscape architect was the American George Hargreaves, whose response was to create a landscape that would compliment the house and associate it with aspects of the Napa Valley environment.

The house is located within a clearing on the highest point of the hill, from where the land falls away into woods of oaks and firs. The landscape that surrounds the site is one of valleys and hills covered with a mix of vineyards and forest. The house is approached by a drive that

Opposite: **Red poppies add a splash of colour in an alien location in Derek Jarman's garden on a beach opposite Dungeness B nuclear power station. The vertical sculptural objects, made from tidal debris, echo the pylons and structures of the industrial landscape beyond.**

climbs upwards from the foot of the rise to end in a circular turning area near the top. Here, a gently stepped, serpentine path leads to the front elevation of the house, which is a white-painted abstract composition of rectilinear and triangular forms. Behind the broad but narrow building, and off centre, is a long, rectangular swimming pool, which terminates in a five-storey tower. On either side of this unusual guesthouse is a projecting flagpole from which hangs a colourful flag.

The pool is contained within an area of paving that is part of a terrace linking the main house to the guest house and the garden's only recreational area. The tower sits on a slightly raised knoll, and it is here that Hargreaves' landscaping begins. Circled around the tower are concentric and contrasting rings of two different and distinct types of perennial grasses. The paler grass bands are a mix of rattlesnake grass with blue flax. The darker bands of taller-growing grasses are created with a combination of fescue and bluegrass, seeded with Californian poppy. The flax and poppies are included to add seasonal colour, and all the grasses are native species and drought-tolerant.

The outer rings of grass around the tower unravel to form serpentine stripes that run back to the main house through the large area of sloping ground and retained trees to the side of the swimming-pool terrace. The stripes re-emerge at the front of the house, their shape mimicking the curving line of the entrance path, as they descend to wrap around the turning circle in the drive. Below the bands of grass, the landscape dissolves into the existing woodland.

Hargreaves' design, with its use of a simple but distinctive grass pattern, mirrors both the contours of the site and the surrounding, undulating landscape; it also makes reference to the more cultivated parts of the region in that the zigzag bands echo the pattern of the vineyards that wind along the sides of the valleys.

A seaside location provides a wealth of inspiration for any designer. The late Derek Jarman created a very special coastal garden around

Alan Everard makes use of wood that has been shaped by the processes of the sea, as well as other discarded maritime objects such as ropes and lobster pots, in his seaside garden at Pevensey Bay in Sussex. The planting in the foreground includes the native yellow horned poppy (*Glaucium flavum*).

Opposite: A gravel path leads past a circle of seashells to a wooden bench decorated with fishing-net floats that were discovered by Naila Green on the adjacent beach. Sited at the point where the garden tumbles over the cliff edge, the bench emphasizes the view, and makes the seascape part of the garden scene.

Designer Naila Green uses plants that are well suited to the location of her garden on a cliff top in Devon. Although not native to the area, many of the plants, such as *Lychnis coronaria*, are closely related to the natural vegetation found along this coast.

his fisherman's cottage on an exposed pebble beach near Lydd in Kent. Prospect Cottage's garden, which has the Dungeness B nuclear power station as a backdrop, is a landscape of totem pole-like sculptures set among shingle, pebbles, and a rich carpet of unexpected plants. Gardens are not usually attempted on beaches, as such sites present difficult growing conditions and reduce the choice of plants. Jarman's garden boasts a surprisingly wide range of plants, including poppies, marigolds, irises, and dog roses, which all seem to thrive in this alien context, alongside the more expected sea kale and santolina.

Jarman's informally arranged clumps of planting echo the hummocks of natural vegetation that stretch across the pebble-strewn beach, and become visible when the tide has retreated. It is a garden created out of the landscape it has adopted, and, by retaining the existing pebble surface, he has made the garden appear to extend out into the tidal beach. The vertical debris sculptures, made from driftwood, rusting metal, and other found objects, provide a contrast to the horizontal lines of the seascape. Their structural and mechanical appearance makes a reference to the industrial landscape of the nearby power station.

The garden does not imitate its surroundings in the literal sense of the word. The mimicry is more symbolic, suggesting and inferring, rather than copying. Jarman once said that his garden's boundaries were the horizon, and here there are no walls or fences. The use of the found materials also relates the garden to the coast, which is shaped and governed by the sea. The debris, weathered and worn and delivered to the garden from far and wide, emphasizes this tidal process.

Another seaside garden, this time designed by the American landscape architect Isabelle C. Greene at Carpentaria, on the Californian

This view of Isabelle C. Greene's beach house garden at Carpentaria, on the Californian coast, appears completely natural. Despite being washed by the sea, however, it is a man-made environment, and the planted rockery and rope-and-wood jetty are all part of the garden.

coast, is also very close to the water. The garden of the beach house begins set back from the ocean, but continues down and on to the shore, to appear as part of it. A rudimentary jetty, a sloping sandy path through rocks, and a planting mix of native and appropriate garden plants combine to mimic the natural surroundings. The result is a design in which it is difficult to see where the seaside garden ends and the actual seashore begins.

High above a beach on a cliff top in Devon is a garden created by garden designer Naila Green. The property at Highover, in Dawlish, boasts a spectacular sea view, providing a formidable backdrop. This is a garden that alludes to its nautical location by subtle touches and a planting style designed to blur the boundary between the garden and its cliff-top surroundings. Views are not obscured, and there is no shelter-belt to protect the garden from the prevailing winds. The planting is dominated by low-growing lavenders and small-leaved silver and grey foliage plants that are drought-tolerant and can withstand the wind. An occasional phormium, agapanthus, or phlomis provides upright accents, and larger-leaved evergreen shrubs, such as fatsia, are kept close to the house. Green's strategy is to allow the wildflowers and grasses of the neighbouring cliff top to self seed and colonize the garden, mixing with the introduced plants.

The garden begins at a patio-style decked area from where it extends outwards, towards and seemingly over, the cliff. Walk-on surfaces are created with shingle (there is no paving), and seashells describe a route that leads to a bench. Perched on the cliff-edge, this resting place is surrounded by items found during Green's beachcombing expeditions. The garden's design is a response to its location, and a combination of indigenous and cultivated planting, with artifacts as reminders of the seascape below.

The deserts of Arizona are where American landscape architect Steve Martino feels most at home. His knowledge of the local vegetation enables him to impersonate the desert landscape when creating gardens there. Just as Julie Toll's wildflower gardens

A reflecting pool stretches out from a walled courtyard garden into the desert landscape surrounding this house in Paradise Valley, Arizona. The desert-like planting beyond the pool is intended to integrate the house with its surroundings, and was conceived by landscape architect Steve Martino.

(*see p. 124*) are not exact copies of an English meadow, so Martino's creations are not slavish imitations of the desert. They cannot ever be exact replicas, since this would entail leaving the land to nature, without control or intervention. Two gardens designed in Arizona by Martino, one for a house in Paradise Valley, the other for the tree nursery Arid Zone Trees (AZT), also in the Sonoran desert region, show how well Martino can integrate a man-made landscape into a natural environment.

The Paradise Valley house was built in 1998 by the owners, the Stitelers. It was inspired by the work of the late Mexican architect Luis Barragán, whose style is readily identifiable by its almost monastic simplicity, and its use of plain walls painted in vivid colours. Martino, who began as an architect before turning to landscape design, is also known for his use of brightly coloured walls to divide spaces and as backdrops to his planting.

At the Stiteler house, Martino's brief was to reclaim the desert and to bring it into the garden. The garden he created is mostly contained within a series of walled spaces and terraces, some of which are quite small, while others are larger and more open. One space is intended as an outdoor dining area and includes a fireplace. In another, a water trough reflects the sky, and a window-like aperture in the colourful sheltering wall frames a view and links the secluded inner garden with the desert landscape beyond. The contained spaces form an intermediate zone between the house and desert.

Wherever possible and practical, Martino chooses plants that are native to the Sonoran or nearby Chihuahuan deserts: species that are well suited to both the local climate and to Martino's naturalistic

At the house in Paradise Valley Martino designed low, coloured walls to form transitional areas between the house and the surrounding desert. The designer uses only plants indigenous to the region, and plants them in a naturalistic manner.

planting schemes. His choice of plants and expert knowledge of plant groupings that occur naturally combine to make his gardens look perfectly at home in their desert setting. Martino's use of isolated specimens or small groups of plants mimics the sparse vegetation of the desert landscape, but he also designs with plants and is keen to highlight their structure or colour. At the Stiteler house, the coloured walls frame his planting compositions in a garden that achieves a balance between the natural and the designed.

Beyond the garden walls Martino has created an entirely naturalistic desert landscape. Although man-made, it is so desert-like that it attracts an abundance of wildlife, including birds and small reptiles. The original site contained a desert "wash", a shallow, natural drainage channel, where vegetation was unusually dense and provided cover for animals. It was destroyed during the preparation work, and Martino was asked to restore it as part of his brief. He did this using his experience in habitat reconstruction gained at the nearby Desert Botanical Garden.

Martino's commission for AZT was to restore a derelict and neglected area of cultivated land to its original, natural splendour. AZT is a nursery that specializes in trees found in desert regions of the United States, including the South West. The idea for the tree farm came from Martino himself, who had found it difficult to find farm-grown trees for his

Right: At the AZT nursery in the Sonoran Desert, a low serpentine wall covered in glossy tiles resembles the form of a snake, but it also makes a seat that connects with a sunken amphitheatre. Designed by Steve Martino, the features combine to form a teaching area within the AZT landscape gardens.

Below: Martino has used sculptural shapes to refer his new landscape to its environment. Here, the curving pointed forms echo the structures of plants that are native to the region, such as agave and opuntia.

projects in desert-derived landscapes. He had suggested the idea to the Douglas family, fruit growers for whom he had previously designed a garden, and they started AZT in 1982. The nursery now produces over 65,000 trees of 59 different species each year.

The completed landscaping for the tree farm includes an entry garden, an arboretum, and spaces allocated for demonstration gardens. The garden at the farm's entrance features a wide range of plants from the Sonoran Desert, including wildflowers and cacti, and these are set against Martino's characteristic, boldly coloured rectangular walls. Around the new farm office, the landscape of trees, and drought-tolerant planting contains serpentine walls and circular enclosures, which are intended as outdoor educational facilities.

A circle of stones makes the entrance to what appears to be a natural and mysterious landscape. In fact, it is a temporary garden created by Mary Reynolds at the Chelsea Flower Show in 2002. Unlike most of the competitors, this garden did not rely on a floral display for its effect.

The construction of the dry-stone walls in Reynolds' "*Tearmann si* – A Celtic Sanctuary" shows great attention to detail, with planting tucked into crevices between the stones to give the illusion that it has been there for years.

The inspiration for Martino's garden designs often comes from the topography of the site, but AZT's location was featureless, so he drew his ideas from a diverse range of visual starting points: the art of early civilizations and the forms associated with ancient monuments, as well as those of plants and reptiles have all inspired the tree farm's gardens. These references can be identified in the garden's amphitheatre-like enclosures and its serpentine walls, clad in iridescent tiles to resemble the skin of a snake. Martino's modern landscape pays homage to the American desert landscape both past and present; its planting is a restoration of the vegetation that once grew there before the original farm was abandoned to become a sandy wasteland.

"Faking it" is the best way to describe the creation of a garden for the Chelsea Flower Show in 2002. Entitled "*Tearmann si* – A Celtic Sanctuary" and designed by Mary Reynolds, this gold-medal-winning garden was a *tour de force* in mimicry. It truly seemed that an ancient piece of the Irish landscape had been dug up and transported to the Chelsea showground.

A "moongate" provided the entrance into a landscape of dry-stone walls and a wild meadow. At its centre was a circular pool containing a stone fireplace. Attention to detail, both in the planting and the man-made features, was the secret of the garden's success. The walls were made to look as if they had been there for years by the squeezing of ferns and mosses into crevices between the stones. The planting was restricted to species commonly found in Ireland, and included four old and gnarled hawthorn trees. Reynolds' studied observation of a real Irish landscape meant that she was able to create a planted environment that appeared to have established itself naturally. The paradox is that this was a convincing recreation of a place that is itself imaginary.

The inspiration for the design of a garden at Portland, Oregon, is much more real and also more eclectic in that it draws upon local, British, and Japanese influences. Much of the west coast of the United States is strongly influenced by Japan and China, and Portland has within its city limits a Japanese and a Chinese public garden. However, the eastern influence in this garden is tempered by the owners' desire to grow and experiment with unusual plants in true plant-collector fashion. The Pacific Northwest has a fairly temperate climate that permits a vast range of plants to grow successfully. In addition, Portland is surrounded by beautiful scenery, which is rich in vegetation and wildflowers.

Norm Kalbfleisch and Neil Matteucci's 0.8-ha (2-acre) garden reveals their inquisitive interest in plants as well as their respect for nature and willingness to adopt diverse styles. The house, designed by American architect Pietro Belluschi, combines the openness of the traditional Japanese home with the classic American porch-fronted shack, and provides its residents with many views on to the surrounding garden.

The living room looks towards a woodland of mature Douglas firs and red cedars which are located outside the property but have been adopted as part of the garden landscape through clever planting schemes. Between the house and the wilderness, Kalbfleisch and Matteucci have planted a mixture of indigenous flowering trees and shrubs, such as wild cherries and rhododendrons. Woodland plants, including many unusual ones such as trilliums and orchids, add to the scene.

The early style of Japanese gardens, characterized by azaleas, magnolias, and cherries placed against a background of evergreens and trees – some part of the surrounding landscape – has been imitated in another part of this garden. Areas of moss and standing stones continue the Japanese theme, which evokes a landscape that is distant both geographically and culturally.

The dense planting in the garden conceals the fence, and this, along with the mimicking of the local vegetation, has enabled the owners to integrate the garden with its surroundings.

This is a view from the house of a garden designed by its owners, Norm Kalbfleisch and Neil Matteucci. The foreground vegetation partially conceals this view, adding a sense of mystery and surprise. A Japanese-inspired landscape is just visible, with indigenous planting forming a backdrop.

Garden as Event

A wooden pier stretches out into the inhospitable and dangerous waters of a swamp in Charleston, S.C. It leads to the swamp garden, a temporary landscape installation designed by West 8 for a festival intended to increase public awareness of the "low country" area.

Since the late 1960s we have seen the emergence of a different type of garden, one instigated not by landscape architects, but by artists. While many artists continue to represent the landscape in painting or photography, over the last 40 years, a number have chosen to leave the comfort of the studio in favour of working more directly with the landscape. The resulting art form, referred to as "land" or "environmental" art, has caused a blurring of the distinction between art and landscape architecture; it has also stimulated a broadening of the concept of what constitutes a garden.

These hybrid landscapes are not always associated with a house, as a garden usually is, but are often created in remote environments. They are rarely permanent but, instead, are frequently temporary installations, created for garden festivals or other special occasions, and they are without boundaries in many senses. Some are without boundaries quite literally, because they are situated within or as part of an existing landscape. Others have no permanent boundaries as they survive for only a short period. All are without boundaries in the conceptual sense, since they expand the definition of the garden beyond its traditional confines.

"The Swamp Garden", created in 1997 by Adriaan Geuze and West 8 Landscape Architects as part of the Spoleto Arts Festival in Charleston, South Carolina, was a garden without boundaries in every sense. It was short-lived, it was located within an existing landscape, it had limited access, and it was a fusion of art and landscape architecture.

The festival includes music, theatre, literature, and the visual arts. In 1997, its theme was "Human/Nature: Art and Landscape in Charleston and the Low Country," and works of art were displayed throughout the city. The West 8 team concentrated on exploiting the special characteristics of their chosen site – a swamp. The lowland swamp, out of which tall cypress trees emerge, is an inhospitable place, and seldom entered into or experienced, despite its inherent beauty. In it, West 8 created what can

In the "Swamp Garden", visitors entered a rectangular chamber defined by walls of Spanish moss suspended from wires. The shimmering light of the semi-opaque curtain contrasted strongly with the dark, gloomy waters of the swamp to create a magical experience.

Previous pages: In the distance, hidden behind the trunks of swamp cypresses, is the "Swamp Garden". While dramatic and distinctive when experienced from inside, the organic structure was almost invisible within the landscape.

Above left: This pond is part of an artwork created by Karen McCoy at a park near Syracuse, N.Y. The lines on the surface of the water are formed by arrowhead plants to echo natural and man-made lines associated with the local landscape.

Above right: The lines in this pond by McCoy are extended into the countryside by cutting and trampling the nearby grass. Some lines, such as this grass labyrinth circle, refer to the way man has marked the landscape.

be best described as cathedral-like. Their construction consisted of a rectangular, architectural structure of steel poles; these were interconnected by horizontal steel wires, over which Spanish moss was draped to form semi-translucent, drapery-like walls. A section of the swamp was set apart and confined by the structure, and the delicacy of the moss walls contrasted with the solid trunks of the cypress trees that were captured within the space. Light filtered through the moss, as though through a stained-glass window, creating a "chamber" that was charged with atmosphere.

A boardwalk led visitors from dry land over the water, through the moss curtain, and along one side of the chamber. A platform projected at right angles as a mooring bay for boats. Two benches made from cypress trunks encouraged visitors to sit and experience the space, which produced a sense of confinement and isolation within the apparently endless, swamp environment.

American artist Karen McCoy was also inspired by a sense of place when she chose to create a temporary landscape at Stone Quarry Hill Art Park in Cazenovia, near Syracuse, New York. McCoy describes her art as "a process of remembering, imagining, and contemplating historical and present-day uses of the land". For her, the ideal way to express her ideas regarding the effects of nature and culture on the landscape is by working with the land itself. The title of McCoy's work at Stone Quarry Hill was "Considering Mother's Mantle", which refers to the thin layer of earth that lies over the bedrock – the part of the landscape that bears the most scars of the conflict between man and nature.

A particularly interesting feature of the area was the way the marsh grasses in a pond grew in clusters along glacial grooves. The work itself developed from McCoy's study of the site, and she noticed that the organic lines of the grasses were echoed in the grid-like lines of nearby fields. She decided to emphasize these lines, and, with the aid of string and a compass, she rearranged arrowhead plants in the pond into lines. She then extended this effect into the surroundings by cutting lines in the grass near the pond and transplanting grass into the adjacent fields. Along the lines, she created other visual events, including a circle of flattened and woven grass. Rich in subtlety, the work was a gentle exploitation of nature connecting the underlying geology of the site to the overlying man-made agricultural landscape. Since McCoy used plants and altered an existing landscape, her artwork could also be described as a garden.

While most gardeners prefer to tend manicured lawns, cultivate garden plants, and keep weeds at bay, the German artist Lois Weinberger

This broken-up area of an asphalt car park represents a "garden in process". It was created by the artist Lois Weinberger for an exhibition in Germany, and he allowed most of the newly exposed ground to be colonized naturally by vegetation.

Lines of white banners hang from wires above a recently deconsecrated area of a cemetery in Lausanne, Switzerland. It is part of "White Flight", a temporary garden created by Atelier Tangente to pay homage to the lives of those whose grave stones once stood there.

is more interested in the wilder, more aggressive, and even toxic types of plants. He prefers the sort of vegetation that can colonize even the most inhospitable places and can return to nature such places as disused industrial sites and railway lines. In Weinberger's "gardens", these neglected and artless plants are celebrated.

"Brennen und Gehen" (Burning and Going) was an art-based landscape created by Weinberger for the Documenta X exhibition in Kassel, central Germany. It was made in a car park, where the artist broke up segments of the tarmac; he then arranged these to form a sort of anarchic rockery, leaving pockets of exposed soil and gravel. He planted a few *Cichorium intybus* but left the remainder of the transformation from car park to garden in the hands of nature and the type of plants that produce seemingly spontaneous vegetation.

It is not only "art parks" and exhibitions that have given rise to new landscapes. The recent phenomenon of the International Garden Festival, an event only ever lasting a few months, has seen the creation of many innovative but temporary gardens. Flower shows, such as the famous Chelsea Flower Show in London, are the forerunners to these, although they tend to be traditional in outlook and predominantly horticultural. It was in Europe, in particular at Chaumont, in France, that a more experimental garden show evolved, and, most recently, at Les Jardins de Métis in

Quebec, Canada, the idea has developed even further. The organizers of these festivals seek work not only from landscape designers but also from artists and architects. Many of the "gardens" created at these festivals have questioned the conventional definition of the garden, and have further blurred the distinction between environmental art and landscape design.

In 2000, the Festival Lausanne Jardin, in Lausanne, Switzerland, proposed four sites within the town for the creation of temporary gardens: one was the Bois de Vaux Cemetery. The nature of this site presented potential participants with a particularly difficult challenge. The festival promoter's aim was to encourage the local inhabitants to visit an often neglected part of the town, but the idea of a cultural event taking place

Above a pool, a stone hangs from each of two balancing devices. When disturbed by the wind, the arms flex, and the stones move up and down over the surface of the water to create a ripple effect. These sculptures feature in a garden that the author designed to symbolize the evolution of life.

"Limed Parterre with Skywriter" by landscape architect Martha Schwartz was conceived as an art installation. The lines on the turf, pass over benches and are only interrupted by trees; they connect with pilasters on the façade to extend it visually into the quadrangle.

in an area specifically reserved for reverence and private memories could also be regarded as insensitive. However, the challenge was accepted by Atelier Tangente, a Swiss-based group of landscape architects.

The management of the cemetery follows a strict sequence: every 25 years the oldest remaining section is deconsecrated, the gravestones are taken away, and the plots are left fallow for a period of time. The ground is then seeded with meadow flowers, and, eventually, the distinct alleys between the original rows of graves disappear. Atelier Tangente's team of Carine Bouvatier, Alice Brauns, and Marion Talagr opted to create a garden in this gravestone-free area of the cemetery. They felt that this section was no longer "exclusively the city of the dead" but a place for the living, like a public park. As a gesture to the former use of the ground, they decided to make a garden that would honour, if only for a short time, those whose names had been erased.

"White Flight", the garden they created, took the form of a series of white, flag-like panels suspended from horizontal wires stretched above where the lines of graves would have been. White, matte, and translucent, these vertically suspended "steles" could move in the wind, catch the light, and cast shadows on the ground, like the stones that had once stood there. The ground under the hanging steles was planted with delicate, shallow rooting green flowers. It was a successful and moving installation – most gardens of remembrance are permanent and formal affairs, but this transient creation was more liberal in its sentiment. It was a garden that respected the past, present, and future.

A garden the author designed at Kilcot in Gloucestershire is a permanent fixture, but its ambitious theme concerns time and the creation of life. It is an allegorical garden, without a boundary in both the real and symbolic senses. It is not confined by fences or walls, and its narrative content comes to no conclusion.

Near a circular pool, a sculpture of a female figure holds an upturned urn from which imaginary water flows. The water, represented by slates set on edge, enters the pond. In the centre of this real pool, and suspended by wires just above the surface, are two stones. These rise and fall with

the wind, "kissing" the surface of the water in the process. The ripples that are formed radiate outwards, forcing the pool's water to spill over into an area of moisture-loving plants. The planting is allowed to develop naturally and without restriction, and placed within it are geometric artifacts, intended to symbolize the arrival of human life in the evolutionary process.

The American landscape architect and artist Martha Schwartz creates both permanent and temporary landscape installations. In 1988 she was asked to design a temporary feature to celebrate the restoration of the Radcliffe residential quadrangle at Harvard University in Cambridge, Massachusetts. The main dormitory, Moors Hall, is located at one end of the rectilinear quadrangle, and its classical façade dominates the space. As part of the renovation, a new cafeteria with a semi-circular front was constructed at the building's base. Projecting outwards, it replaced the original formal classical-style terrace. This change, and additional alterations to the lawn, meant that the architectural detail of the building was no longer connected visually to the floor of the quadrangle.

Schwartz's scheme aimed to resurrect this relationship between the classical-style building and landscape of the quadrangle. Her solution, entitled "Limed Parterre with Skywriter", started from the six existing pilasters on the front of the hall and inventively extended them into the landscape. Firstly, lines were painted over the roof terrace and down the front of the cafeteria, then bands of hand-applied lime were drawn across the lawn, through the car park and into the street. Above the lawn, and aligned over the painted and lime stripes, six parallel vapour trails were created artificially at intervals during the day.

Schwartz's garden "event" at Harvard highlights the association that has recently developed between garden design and art forms such as land art and installation art. Schwartz has been influenced by American

Above: **A group of Canadian artists known as BGL created this unusual structure, entitled "Sentier Battu", at the 2001 Festival International de Jardins at Métis in Quebec. This view under their canopy of wire and green tape allows a glimpse of the sky and trees, but mainly focuses attention on the destruction on the woodland floor.**

Right: **This shows an overview of the wire-and-tape roof from a specially created aerial platform. The delicate green surface suggests a small landscape that merges with the foliage of the surrounding trees. The sight of visitors beneath the mesh can be quite disconcerting.**

land artists such as Michael Heizer and Robert Smithson. At Radcliffe, she created a landscape that challenged the traditional concept that assumes that a garden is a long-term project.

Schwartz's idea of using space both on and above the ground has been capitalized upon by a small group of artists in Quebec who work under the collective name of BGL. Individually they are: Jasmin Bilodeau, Sébastien Gigure, and Nicolas Laverdière. They created their "twin-level" garden for the Festival International de Jardins 2001, held at Les Jardins de Métis in Quebec.

The three artists met while studying visual arts at Quebec's Université Laval. Their art, which usually takes the form of installations, involves the recovery and recycling of used materials in unexpected ways. For

their garden at Métis they turned to new materials, but chose to use only those that are commonplace and designed to serve another more utilitarian functions.

"Sentier Battu", BGL's home-made, temporary garden, was situated within a clearing in a woodland, and consisted of a suspended canopy made from thousands of short pieces of green adhesive tape attached to over one hundred nylon wires. The sheer density of the lines of tape swatches stretching across the site created the impression of a quivering and shimmering ceiling. Beneath the shade of this synthetic, translucent roof was a desolate, debris-littered world, containing the remains of felled trees. The "garden" could be viewed from ground level and via a purpose-built platform from above. The relationship between the two environments – one plastic and airborne, the other a landscape of man-made destruction – can be interpreted in both political and environmental terms, but the visual impact of the work, viewed from above or below, was sufficiently satisfying in itself.

At the Festival International de Jardins in the same year, the Canadian architect Pierre Thibault collaborated with Katherine McKinnon and Vadim Siegal to create a piece called "Jardin Territoire". In their unusual garden, the St Lawrence seaway shoreline, with its natural and geological

Left: A canal separates two areas dedicated to growing wheat in this garden called "Jardin Territoire", created by Canadian architect Pierre Thibault at the garden festival at Métis in Canada in 2001. The garden was inspired by the history of the landscape surrounding the festival site.

Right: The stepping-stone paths in Thibault's garden are made from slices of timber from the local area. They are more clearly seen before the wheat has grown up.

history, was reconstructed in an environment of tall-growing cultivated plants. A channel of water was used to represent the primordial sea or river. Arranged on either side of this central feature were samples of plant material or mineral matter that had been taken from a number of nearby locations, including the salt marsh, the tidal flats, the shoreline, and a furrow of cultivated wheat. The "samples" of land, living or fossil, were lifted from their natural setting and transported to the site, where they were inserted into the garden space. The surrounding landscape had quite literally been borrowed.

At the Métis festival in 2002, the Italian LAND-I, the Roman architects and landscape designers Marco Antonini, Roberto Capecci, and Raffaella Sini created a garden of "holes". They sank 49 identical, rectangular

"Ombre" (Shadow) was the title of the LAND-I contribution to the 2002 Métis festival. Rectangular steel chambers without bases were inserted into a landscape stripped of vegetation. The only planting is in the "shadow" of the troughs in this mysterious and thought-provoking landscape.

openings into a flat, plantless landscape set among trees. The work was called "Ombre" ("Shadow" in French) and, according to the designers, it was a garden about two types of shadow: those that define form by the effects of light and shade, and the more enigmatic sort that are not so visible but can reveal the history of a site. The holes were arranged in a random pattern, and at the base of each sunken steel coffin-like rectangle, at a depth of 60cm (24in), were placed "shadow"-tolerant, ground-cover plants. The 49 excavations were intended to suggest that an ancient garden once lay beneath the present surface.

It is hard to determine whether these festival landscapes are gardens or artworks. Since plants are used, there is the suggestion of traditional garden, but, as with everything else, these creations are disposed of when the festival closes. Such gardens are perhaps best understood as a temporary, yet appropriate means of expressing visual ideas concerning the living environment.

The transitory existence of installation-style festival gardens is highlighted by the fact that they will have been destroyed long before the plants have grown to maturity. In contrast, at the five-day Chelsea Flower Show the use of fully grown or mature specimens to create instant gardens is expected and required. The British garden designer Bonita Bulaitis had the best of both worlds when she was asked to create a long-term garden-installation at King's Heath Park in Birmingham, England. Commissioned by the BBC for its "Gardeners' World" television series, it was one of three demonstration gardens built in the park.

The garden is as much art park as landscape, dominated as it is by a number of free-standing, orange "sculptures". Each sculpture consists of interlocking triangular walls or planes, some pierced with a matrix of small holes, others featuring larger porthole-like apertures. The sculptures

Top and above: **These are two views of a garden created by Bonita Bulaitis at King's Heath Park. A series of interlocking, boldly coloured triangular forms lead visitors through the garden space. The sculptural structures conceal part of the garden from immediate view, while the circular apertures draw the attention to particular trees or shrubs.**

This aerial view of a project created for Pagago Park/City Boundary by Steve Martino and Jody Pinto shows how dry-stone walls make the shape of a simple tree. The trunk receives the water that spills out to fill the spaces defined by its branches. As the land is irrigated, so the "tree" will change from a wintry skeleton to a living sculpture, abundant with greenery, turning this derelict piece of land into a garden.

are placed within a landscape of restrained planting and grey gravel, and against a backdrop of the park's existing trees and meadowland. Orange-coloured timbers, set into the gravel in a diagonal, parallel formation, identify the pathway that runs through the garden.

The sculptural features are important, since they guide the visitor through the space, and provide a three-dimensional element that is lacking in many gardens. In addition, because the garden is not adjacent to a building, their wall-like appearance provides an architectural point of reference. They give the garden an identity that allows it to exist as a landscape in its own right, without the need for a reassuring building. By acting as divisions within the space, the sculptures also conceal parts of the site from view to provide an element of surprise. The large circular holes allow a glimpse of what lies on the other side and frame plants that deserve thew viewers's special attention.

The planting is natural in appearance. Silver birches are used to link the garden with the park beyond the site, and grasses, including the feathery *Stipa tenuissima* and small-leaved, bronze sedges, play a large part. The stronger forms of *Phormium* 'Bronze Baby' provide contrast, while the boldly painted walls act as a foil to the texture and colour of the planting. On a practical level, the walls also provide pockets for those plants that require a more sheltered environment.

As with many of Bulaitis's other projects, this garden started life as a three-dimensional model. Her working practice is more akin to that of a sculptor, who will develop the spatial aspect of a work through a series of maquettes before committing the design to bronze, stone, or steel. It is as a result of Bulaitis's adherence to this process that the design for King's Heath Park has such a three-dimensional quality. The central sculptural forms allow it to be enjoyed from a multiplicity of viewpoints and negate the need for an obvious boundary.

An environmental project for Pagago Park/City Boundary in Phoenix, Arizona, also has a strong sculptural feel. The landscape, situated away from buildings, is defined on two of its sides by major roads that meet at the corner of the site. Completed in 1992 and designed by New York-based artist Jody Pinto, in association with landscape architect Steve Martino, it is essentially an interconnected arrangement of dry-stone walls, which resembles a tree from the air.

The central trunk of the tree is a straight wall, which is terminated at its broadest end by two stone pillars and aligned so as to "connect" two local communities. The trunk wall contains a channel to harvest rainwater. The collected water pours from openings positioned along the

This the central trunk of the tree-shaped landscape project created for Pagago Park/City Boundary by Martino and Pinto. Rainwater pours from a trough located within a wall and floods defined areas of lifeless desert land.

A dry-stone wall weaves its way through a woodland landscape and disappears into the mist at Grizedale Forest in Cumbria. This is not a functional wall as it does not define land boundaries, but is an artwork by British artist Andy Goldsworthy.

length of the channel to fill areas that are defined by the stone tree's curving branch walls. The intention of the project is to regenerate 0.8ha (2 acres) of eroded desert land. What was once an area devoid of life is now colonized by planting.

Over the centuries, the natural landscape has been shaped by human intervention. While some people have sought to establish cultivated gardens for leisure and pleasure, others have simply transformed existing landscapes, creating art as a part of their daily lives and rituals, rather than to serve a specific function. Neither connected to a building nor enclosed, these latter landscapes are truly without boundaries. A follower of this style, the British artist Andy Goldsworthy has embarked on projects to transform existing landscapes. He is known for making temporary artworks from natural materials, and for working with dry-stone walling. In the 1980s, he accepted an offer to create a number of sculptures for the Grizedale Forest Sculpture Trail in Cumbria.

One of his works, entitled "Taking a Wall for a Walk" is inspired by the local tradition of dry-stone wall building. Walls of this type, using local stone, have long been built throughout the region to define land boundaries. They climb up and down the mountains of Cumbria and are still constructed today. Goldsworthy employed a local team of skilled wall makers to construct his snaking dry-stone wall, which weaves through the Grizedale Forest for some 137m (500ft). It avoids trees, rather than demolishes them, and embraces the forest landscape through a series of openings and closures. In this way, Goldsworthy gives this part of the seemingly endless and repetitive forestry planting an identity, and a sense of place.

Goldsworthy completed several other large environmental works at Grizedale Forest during his residency there. One of the most impressive is "Seven Spires", a response to his feelings at being within a pine forest, his awareness of what he calls an "almost desperate growth and energy driving upward". Each tree-height "spire" was formed by gripping together numerous lengths of felled tree trunks to make a slender conical form. The stacks are clustered deep in the pine forest, and with their heavenwards-surging, architectural lines, they evoke the ambience of a cathedral.

Standing within their presence is spiritually uplifting; like the wall, this work establishes a sense of place within the forest's anonymous vastness.

Another British artist, David Nash, has earned a reputation for creating art from both cut and living wood and, like Goldsworthy, has created works in Grizedale Forest. Nash used two fallen trees and a natural water source to create an unusual water feature as one of his contributions to the sculpture trail. His "Wooden Waterway" belongs where it was created. A natural spring supplies the water that is diverted along two branch-troughs. The water then runs through the roots of a fallen oak, down its trunk, off along an ash branch-trough, through the roots of a fallen sycamore, down its trunk, and, finally, along more branches to eventually disappear from sight under a stone. "Wooden Waterway" is an inventive and sensitive use of the natural landscape, and it transforms an area of woodland debris into a water garden without boundaries.

David Nash and Andy Goldsworthy are first and foremost artists. They have ventured into the forest to use what they discover to create art that is both of and in the landscape. By working with the land in this way they unintentionally create what could also be described as gardens.

Opposite: Towering and tapering columns of felled timber soar into the conifer canopy. This artwork by Andy Goldsworthy is intended to heighten our awareness of the space in which it exists and to create a sense of place within the blanket planting of the man-made forest.

Below: Artist David Nash has created an unusual water feature by connecting a natural spring to a series of channels cut into fallen trees. His "Wooden Waterway" takes advantage of materials that are already available in the landscape, rather than introducing alien ones.

Index

Page references in *italics* refer to illustrations

Acknowledgments

Mitchell Beazley would like to acknowledge and thank the following for supplying photographs for inclusion in this book.

Endpapers Nicola Browne; half title, 2, 5 Harpur Garden Library/Jerry Harpur, 8 Bridgeman Art Library, 9 Harpur Garden Library/Jerry Harpur, 10 Bridgeman Art Library/Giraudon, 11 Garden Picture Library/John Glover, 12 Garden Picture Library/Lamontagne, 13 Nicola Browne, 14–15 Andrew Lawson Photography, 16-17 Garden Matters/John Feltwell, 18 © Eames Office 2002, www.eamesoffice.com, photo Tim Street-Porter, 19 Arcaid/Lewis Gasson, 20 Harpur Garden Library/Jerry Harpur, 21 Rich Haag Associates, 22-23 Garden Exposures Photo Library/Andrea Jones, 24 Richard Davies, 25 Hargreaves Associates, 28, 29 A E Bye Associates, photo A E Bye, 30, 31 Marianne Majerus, 32 Steve Martino & Associates,33 Harpur Garden Library/Jerry Harpur, 35 above and below Steve Martino & Associates, 36, 37 Esto Photographics/Jeff Goldberg, 38, 39 Harry Seidler & Associates, artist Ms Berman, 40, 41 Marianne Majerus, 42–43 Harpur Garden Library/Jerry Harpur, 44, 45 BBC Good Homes Magazine, photos Tim Yang, 46, 47 Stephen Stimson Associates, 48, 49 Nicola Browne, 50 Marianne Majerus, 51 Andrew Lawson Photography, 52–53 Oehme and Van Sweden Associates, photo James Van Sweden, 56–57 SWA Group, 58-59 Andrew Lawson Photography, 60 Marianne Majerus, sculptor Yu Ming, 61 Marianne Majerus, 62 Isabelle Greene & Associates, Santa Barbara, 63 Raymond Jungles Inc, 64–65 Harpur Garden Library/Jerry Harpur, 66, 67 Jonathan Buckley, 68 Nicola Browne, 69 Jonathan Buckley, design Stephanie Grimshaw, 70, 71 Marianne Majerus, 72, 73 Le Scanff-Mayer, 74–75 Jonathan Buckley, 76 Sunniva Harte, 77 Marianne Majerus, 78 David Stevens, design Curtice Taylor, 79 Curtice Taylor, 80 Dani Karavan, photo Alex Rubischon, 84 Child Associates Inc, 85 courtesyJanis Hall, photo Janis Hall, 86 courtesy Janis Hall, landscape architects Bye and Herrmann, photo A E Bye, 87 courtesy Janis Hall, photo A E Bye, 88 Marianne Majerus, design Will Woodhouse, 89 Harpur Garden Library/Jerry Harpur, 90–91 Nicola Browne, 91 Office of H Keith Wagner, 92 Harpur Garden Library/Jerry Harpur, 93 Oehme and Van Sweden Associates, photo James Van Sweden, 94 Balthazar Korab Ltd, design Randall K Metz, 95 Grissim/Metz Associates, photo Roger Foley, 96, 97 Charles Mann Photography Inc, design Julia Berman, Andrew Ungerleider and Gay Dillingham, 98 Garden Picture Library/Ron Sutherland, 99 Olson Sundbery Kundig Allen Architects, photo Dick Busher, 100–101 Arcaid/Alan Weintraub, 104–105 Child Associates Inc, 106 above and below Tim Hursley,107 PLANT, 108–109 Germán del Sol, 110–111 Patrick Bingham Hall, 112 Margherita Spiluttini, 113 SE Group, 114–115 Salmela Architect, landscape architect Coen + Partners, photo Peter Bastianelli Kerze, 116, 117 Siren Arkkitehdit Oy, 118 The Office of Lawrence Halprin Inc, 119 Rich Haag Associates, 120 Arcaid/Mark Fiennes, sculpture Ian Hamilton Finlay, 121 Andrew Lawson Photography, sculpture Ian Hamilton Finlay, 124–5 Marianne Majerus, 126 Fernando Caruncho, 127 Lutsko Associates, 128, 129, 130 Louisa Jones, 131 Marianne Majerus, 132 Harpur Garden Library/Jerry Harpur, design Juan Grimm for J & M Mulville, 133 Harpur Garden Library/Jerry Harpur, design John Brookes for J & M Mulville, 134–5 Arcaid/Richard Waite, 136 Garden Picture Library/John Glover, 137 Sunniva Harte, 138, 139 Nicola Browne, 140–1, 142, 143 Harpur Garden Library/Jerry Harpur, 144, 145 Charles Mann Photography Inc, 146 Jane Sebire, 147 Garden Picture Library/Suzie Gibbons, 148–9 Garden Exposures/Andrea Jones, 152, 153, 154-5 West 8 Urban Design and Landscape Architecture bv, photos Jeroen Musch, 156 left and right Karen McCoy, 157 Lois Weinberger, photo Werner Maschmann, 158 Atelier Tangente, 159 Marianne Majerus, 160–1 Martha Schwartz Inc, photo David Walker, 162, 163, 164, 165, 166 Jean-Claude Hurni,167 above and below Nicola Browne, 168 Steve Martino & Associates, 169 Nicola Browne, 170–1 Andrew Lawson Photography, 172, 173 Grizedale Arts.